FRENCH WINE
CHÂTEAUX

FRENCH WINE CHÂTEAUX

DISTINCTIVE VINTAGES AND THEIR ESTATES

FOREWORD BY CHRISTOPHE NAVARRE
FOREWORD BY DANIEL RONDEAU

TEXT BY ALAIN STELLA
PHOTOGRAPHY BY FRANCIS HAMMOND

Flammarion

7 FOREWORD CHRISTOPHE NAVARRE

8 FOREWORD DANIEL RONDEAU

15 MOËT & CHANDON

45 MERCIER

63 DOM PÉRIGNON

91 VEUVE CLICQUOT

123 KRUG

155 RUINART

179 HENNESSY

211 CHÂTEAU CHEVAL BLANC

243 CHÂTEAU D'YQUEM

FOREWORD

French Wine Châteaux opens the doors to the private wine estates owned by Moët Hennessy and LVMH. Located in the heart of the glamorous French vineyard regions, these wine and spirit makers in Champagne, Bordeaux, Sauternes, and Cognac all boast strong local traditions and unique skills. They were all founded by visionary men and women, and all incarnate a priceless heritage. Despite these shared features, each one has its own genetic imprint, its own authenticity. The oldest of these châteaux dates back to the sixteenth century, for Château d'Yquem was founded in 1593. Most of the others were founded in the eighteenth century, soon winning the favor of Europe's royal and imperial courts. The rise of these houses, built on the foundations of amazing family sagas, continued into the nineteenth and twentieth centuries, displaying remarkable vitality even today.

Moët & Chandon, Dom Pérignon, Mercier, Veuve Clicquot, Krug, Ruinart, Hennessy, Château Cheval Blanc, and Château d'Yquem are brands now recognized throughout the world as the mark of refined taste, thanks to their wonderfully artful blends, or *assemblages*, that create an unforgettably elegant effect on nose and palate. These châteaux also share a long tradition of hosting distinguished visitors who enjoy their marvelous nectars, which have become synonymous with the French art of entertaining. The châteaux call upon talented chefs who excel in creating new combinations of wine and food, elaborated in enthusiastic teamwork with cellar masters and wine tasters. This approach perfectly reflects the reasons why UNESCO has now listed "the French gastronomic meal" as part of humanity's Intangible Cultural Heritage.

This book offers a personal insight into French culture, taking readers into the special world of wine châteaux where the history of refined, gastronomic French winemaking is still being written in the present.

CHRISTOPHE NAVARRE
President and CEO, Moët Hennessy

PAGES 4–5: *A view of the vineyards at Château Cheval Blanc*
in Saint-Émilion from the top of the new winery designed by Christian de Portzamparc.
FACING PAGE: *The former private residence in Reims known as the hôtel du Marc,*
where Veuve Clicquot receives distinguished guests today,
is the perfect incarnation of a sophisticated lifestyle.

FOREWORD
DANIEL RONDEAU
Author, French ambassador to UNESCO

I t was my fate to be born in Mesnil-sur-Oger, a village in Champagne. The local area known as Côte des Blancs seemed to me to be a "metaphor of the world"—a place where I could commune with distant horizons. My great-grandfather had been the village cooper, and my grandfather a winegrower. I loved to watch him work in his storeroom, a vast space with a window overlooking the street, connected to the cellar by a trap door with a rope-and-pulley system for raising and lowering bottles of wine in wicker baskets.

My grandfather soon included me in the grand cycle of working the vineyards and wine, paced by the seasons. I accompanied him to the plots during the periods of plowing and pruning, I climbed into the tuns before the grape-picking, I drank the sweet wine as it ran from the press, and I joined him in the storeroom when champagne was disgorged, watching as he grabbed a bottle, tilted the neck downward, steadied it against his blue apron and struck off the clip retaining the cork with his knife: a cloud of wine vapor swirled around him, scenting the storeroom.

At seventeen I went looking for a vacation job. My grandfather said he knew someone who knew someone who "worked at Moët." That is how I acquired the habit, over a number of years, of spending the summer before returning to high school (and, later, college) by working for that old establishment on Avenue de Champagne in Épernay. I immediately felt at home with Moët & Chandon, a champagne house that was welcoming in more ways than one. It soon became "my" house—I liked to dive deep into the cellars, flashlight in hand, inhaling the odor of wine. Moving down the lanes of that underground city felt like exploring the mysteries of a hidden treasure.

I discovered how tradition was placed at the service of excellence, a tradition that crowned both know-how and savoir-faire. Forty years on, Moët & Chandon is still "my" house (a miracle not just of fidelity but of renewed friendships), even though its star has continued to rise among the constellation of stellar makers of champagne.

Now Moët is flanked by a galaxy of champagne houses, each as glamorous as the next: Dom Pérignon (which has consistently acquired greater strength, subtlety, and wisdom), Mercier (its ever-dynamic former rival), Veuve Clicquot (famous not only for its Clicquot yellow and the oldest attested vintage champagne—1810—but also for its tirelessly ability to rejuvenate itself), Ruinart (obviously), and Krug (whose walled vineyards are one of the prides of Mesnil-sur-Oger). This constellation of champagnes has forged crucial alliances with other prestigious names in other vineyards. Hennessy, the cognac that rediscovered "Paradis" has now become inseparably linked with the name of Moët. And the presence of Château d'Yquem and Château Cheval Blanc on the new map drawn by LVMH group proves that the minds behind these marriages have always had the word "excellence" at heart.

All these companies share a common source of history and tradition that draws strength from local soil and climate as well as the vital skills of the people working the vineyards. Their priceless treasure is the land (humus, chalk, stones, sand, natural springs, plus slope of ground and angle of sunshine). Nature, as sparkling as she is generous, has provided for everything. Everything here exists on a human scale, size, and reach. The land is a palimpsest of countless possibilities, but we should not forget that its history

---

FACING PAGE: *The great saga of vine and wine has been jointly written over the centuries by climate, soil, winemakers, cellar masters, merchants, and, of course, wine lovers.*

has been written by human beings. The winegrower remains at the heart of a battle that mobilizes telluric forces—sun, the all-important wind, the water from springs and rain, the stretch of hills, the pace of seasons, and the vastness of the sky. At Yquem, the land slopes and the soil lacks wealth; in Champagne, the vines are tested every winter by hard frosts, and snowfall is not uncommon. So we owe a great debt to the work of the winegrowers, the cellar masters, the oenologists, the managers, and the owners. Not only have they managed to uncover—and preserve—the treasure that nature had entrusted to the hands of their forefathers, but they have extended and protected it, generation after generation.

They have all contributed—and still contribute—to a collective project that spans the centuries. The role of time can be sensed in the cellars at Moët, to mention those I know best, in the gloom of certain vaults and the solemn beauty of others where old lamps cast a flickering light that must be similar to that which once lit the way for Napoleon Bonaparte, among rows of racks holding bottles in old, petrified shapes. The greatest triumph of all these wine châteaux is to make the flawless nectars that leave their cellars appear so obvious. At the same time, they have drawn the world's attention to these particular patches of land. But the world's heart was not conquered in a day. Time and history have been on the winemakers' side. Champagne was the wine drunk at the coronations of French kings, and the westward road that linked Champagne to Paris and Versailles was an umbilical cord to the royal court, and thence to power. In the nineteenth century champagne became the wine *par excellence* of a country called upon by history to play a worldwide role. The prestige of the grand houses of champagne became international. I remember how astonished I was, some time ago, to discover in Fortnum & Mason on Piccadilly in London a display devoted to Mesnil-sur-Oger and champagne made by Krug. The whole world's undying infatuation with champagne soon opened the way for other fine products from France.

The history of every one of these firms is the story of the men and women who founded and transformed them. Their family tales are packed with remarkable characters—winegrowers, wine merchants, landowners—who often crossed paths with leading figures of the day, as exemplified by the correspondence between Thomas Jefferson, American ambassador to France in the late 1780s, and comte de Lur Saluces, the owner of Yquem. These letters tell us that Jefferson had his own initials engraved on the bottles he ordered and that it was he himself who convinced President George Washington of the qualities of "the white wine of Sauternes." Meanwhile, it was Talleyrand, the French ambassador to the court of Saint James, who taught courtiers in London how to appreciate the finest cognacs from the house of Hennessy. And Jean-Remy Moët's encounters with Napoleon and, later, Tsar Alexander of Russia, are worthy of a work of fiction. Finally, the way in which the famous widow Clicquot managed to corner the Russian market to the point where *klikofksoy* was briefly a synonym for champagne is a saga that goes beyond the bounds of simple trade.

And the saga continues. Every one of these winemakers is keen to preserve its heritage. By "heritage" I do not mean only the glamorous properties— residences, châteaux, cellars, storerooms, grape baskets, and presses—but also the invisible heritage, wherein lies their true wealth. Intelligent efforts are constantly being made to retain and to improve upon traditional skills. Michelin-starred chefs work with winemakers and wine specialists to find wonderful combinations of food and wine. Senior management makes a point of cultivating French savoir-faire— I have seen how conscientiously they work at being perfect hosts who know how to receive, to share, and to celebrate around a table. It is no coincidence that UNESCO has now listed the "French gastronomic meal" as part of the world's Intangible Cultural Heritage. France remains an influential nation in terms of history, politics, economics, literature, and art. But it is above all a welcoming nation that knows how to give of its best when entertaining friends. All the châteaux that I invite you to discover— or rediscover—in this volume share, each in its own way, that French spirit.

PAGES 10–11: *These vineyards on the slopes of Côte des Blancs in Champagne are ranked* grand cru *and are famous for their Chardonnay grapes, which bring all their lightness, finesse, and floral aroma to sparkling champagne.*
FACING PAGE: *Time plays its role in the limestone vaults of Moët & Chandon's wine cellars—bottles of still wine are "trellised" (stacked in alternating rows on wooden slats) while they slowly acquire their effervescence.*

Champagne

MOËT & CHANDON

Champagne

On the banks of the Marne River, nestled between the Montagne de Reims and the hills known as Côte des Blancs, the charming town of Épernay prides itself on being home to numerous grand champagne houses. All along its broad main boulevard—appropriately named Avenue de Champagne—stand a series of sometimes quite lavish mansions, now transformed into the headquarters of glamorous firms. One such firm has premises on both sides of the avenue. On one side is the harmonious image of two large, identical pavilions (one of which is called the "Trianon," where Moët & Chandon hosts private receptions), plus a formal garden and an orangery; opposite is an elegant late eighteenth-century residence of white stone, the Hôtel Moët. This latter, adorned with a fine landscape garden, is linked to a large building reconstructed between 1928 and 1934 on the site of an earlier one destroyed by bombs during World War I. This graceful yet monumental complex is the visible tip of a kingdom that includes seventeen miles of cellars, the domain of one of the most famous champagnes, Moët & Chandon. Ever since its early marketing exploits in the eighteenth century, Moët & Chandon's main goal has been to sell the finest quality champagne. The firm's power and grandeur are exclusively oriented toward a quest for excellence. In what is a highly competitive environment, that means always attaining the top rank, which itself means displaying boldness and innovation. That is how the champagne house manages to distinguish itself with majesty and splendor.

This particular spirit was probably born at the same time as the company itself, in the 1740s at the court of Louis XV. Claude Moët, the younger son of an old family of drapers in Reims, managed a vineyard a few miles from Épernay, where his wife was born and where he moved in 1717. Moët bought a wine brokerage, then opened his own trading house in 1743. The finest of the wines he shipped—most of them to Paris—were delivered in glass bottles. And some of these "sparkling white wines" found their way to the court. In 1750 Moët's diary first mentions the name of his most famous customer, Madame de Pompadour, née Jeanne Antoinette Poisson, who became the king's favorite and was elevated to the rank of marquise in 1745. A witty, cultivated epicurean and an archetypal figure of the enlightenment, Madame de Pompadour liked to declare that "only champagne leaves women beautiful after drinking it."

She adored every new delicacy, from champagne to chocolate (with which she allegedly washed down celery and truffle soup). She was also fond of literature (encouraging Diderot and the Encyclopedists) and architecture (supervising construction of the Petit Trianon); she also enjoyed the romantic and political, if sometimes cruel, plotting that was the daily fare of court life. Every year, when the beautiful marquise traveled north to Compiègne for the summer season, she ordered 120 bottles of Monsieur Moët's finest champagne. Better still, on May 13, 1750, Moët dispatched no fewer than 245 bottles in two crates to the royal residence in Compiègne. From that time onward Moët champagnes have always sparkled in delicate crystal glasses in all the royal courts and high society salons of Europe.

Claude Moët's son, Claude-Louis-Nicolas, maintained the firm's reputation for quality, while his grandson, Jean-Remy, set out to conquer the world. Born in 1758, Jean-Remy made voyages that contributed to the international expansion of the house of Moët, which he inherited on the death of his father in 1792. His early decisions reveal the far-sighted intelligence of the man who would ensure the true grandeur of the company. In the revolutionary France of 1792, developing a coherent business was an exploit indeed. In the midst of political turmoil he took one crucial decision: that the whole of the company's efforts should now focus on the sparkling wine of Champagne, on improving its quality and on extending its reputation. Bolstered by his faith in modernity and progress, he studied the fermentation and maturation of champagne with the eye of a scientist, constantly experimenting with new techniques to reinforce the quality of his creations, and writing theses on the champagne method. "We have to put our heads through torture to achieve beauty," he wrote.

Every year, when Madame de Pompadour traveled north to Compiègne for the summer season, the beautiful marquise ordered 120 bottles of Monsieur Moët's finest champagne.

Gradually the other, more traditional wines once sold by the Moët family were abandoned.

Another crucial decision Jean-Remy made was to move his residence and business to the outskirts of Épernay, on Faubourg de la Folie (which would be renamed Rue du Commerce and then, in 1925, Avenue de Champagne), and he henceforth concentrated solely on sparkling white wine, that is to say, champagne. The lavish home he built in 1793 was designed to do more than merely flaunt the success of the Moët family, for Jean-Remy was one of the first champagne merchants to realize that one of the keys to his success lay in the art of receiving customers, suppliers, and distributors. Champagne is not simply a product like any other, but is a festive beverage to be shared with joy, among family and friends. This is the way to make people love it. So by the 1790s the company began cultivating the art of hosting guests, an art it would refine to perfection and maintain into the present day. A decade later, in 1802, Jean-Remy Moët became mayor of Épernay and had the chance to welcome important visitors to his town, who then became his customers. Visiting celebrities included the Emperor Napoleon, royal princes, diplomats, and wealthy businessmen, who traveled the road between Paris and eastern Europe and found a stopover at the Moët residence to be particularly pleasant.

FACING PAGE: *The Moët residence, in Épernay, built on what is now called Avenue de Champagne, houses offices and reception rooms (top). Under the benevolent gaze of Jean-Remy Moët (1758–1841), cellar master Benoît Gouez strives to perpetuate the stylistic identity of Moët et Chandon Impérial, renowned worldwide since 1895 (bottom).*
PAGE 20: *Chef Bernard Dance devised a sweet Tagada Strawberry charlotte infused with mint, the better to bring out the fragrant notes of fruit, mild spices, mint, and anisette associated with the Grand Vintage Rosé 2002 served at the Trianon.*
PAGE 21: *Madame de Pompadour loved champagne. Concerned about her complexion, she declared that "only champagne leaves women beautiful after drinking it." Every year, just before the onset of summer, Claude Moët recorded in his ledger the 120 bottles that he delivered to Madame de Pompadour at her holiday château in Compiègne.*

Jean-Remy was fully aware that such guests would become his finest ambassadors and, in 1805, he started construction of two new pavilions, with gardens and orangery, called the Trianon and the hôtel Chandon. The pavilions were primarily designed for his children's use, but they also meant he could receive powerful guests in more comfort. Napoleon, already a loyal client, reportedly stayed there in 1807 and again in 1814. The firm went on to celebrate this friendship later, with the addition of the "Impérial" label to its champagnes in 1863.

To spread the reputation of his champagne, Jean-Remy did not just receive people, he also secured the services of wine merchants in the major capitals. He set up a network of sources all over Europe, who kept him informed of everything from changing tastes to the political climate. He selected his "missionaries" with care. Candidates had to be motivated, competent, experienced, and have a good grasp of foreign languages. He sent them out across the continent with samples of his products for which they were instructed to organize tastings. This is how under his name and impetus, this exceptional wine, which was formerly no more than a local specialty, rose to become a universal model.

In 1816, Jean-Remy' son-in-law, Pierre-Gabriel Chandon, was drawn into the business and soon had a stake in the company's performance. Chandon was a son of a lawyer from Mâcon, and a friend and relative of the poet Lamartine. He became all the more important to the firm in so far as Jean-Remy's own son, Victor, had put off joining the business. The two men got on well together and ultimately went into partnership, founding the house of Moët & Chandon in 1833. By the time Jean-Remy retired to his château in Romont—having made his fortune—the firm was by far the largest champagne merchant. It also grew its own grapes on fifty acres of vineyards located on some of the finest land. Moët & Chandon sold roughly two hundred thousand bottles per year, and its cellars held another five hundred thousand bottles. The fame of the quality of its champagnes already stretched from London to Saint Petersburg via Vienna and Prague.

And yet it was in the latter half of the nineteenth century that the company enjoyed its most rapid growth, thanks to the economic boom of France's Second Empire. The new railroad running from Paris to Strasbourg, which opened in 1852, passed through Épernay. By the early 1880s, fifty years after Jean-Remy retired, Moët & Chandon employed over 1,000 people and sold two and a half million bottles per year. Having built up a highly efficient network of agents throughout the world, the firm exported nearly 90 percent of its output. It had responded perfectly to demands for a less sweet wine, with less added sugar, and was able to diversify its range. In 1865, it launched an "extra dry" champagne, called White Star, which would later make Moët & Chandon famous in America once prohibition was repealed. In order to fulfill the growing demand, the company considerably expanded its vineyards, which totaled over 1,200 acres once the private estates of Victor Moët and Pierre-Gabriel Chandon were included. Finally, from the 1850s onward, it began directly buying grapes, rather than wine, in order to control the entire chain of production and maintain full command over quality.

From London to Saint Petersburg, Moët champagnes have always sparkled in delicate crystal glasses in all the royal courts and high society salons of Europe.

FACING PAGE: *On a springtime afternoon, a vineyard hut crowns the Moët-owned slopes of vines ranked* grand cru *on the famous Côte des Blancs near Cramant.*

By the end of the nineteenth century, the Moët & Chandon name was known on every continent, and its champagnes were easily recognizable thanks to the printed labels that had appeared at the dawn of that century. Advertising also played a role in the company's fame. As early as 1860 Moët & Chandon became aware of the importance of this tool of communication and willingly allocated a sizeable budget to it. Famous artists were hired to produce posters, including one of the leading art nouveau designers, Alphonse Mucha. And in 1886, the brand's visible, distinctive emblem—the famous black ribbon with red seal—first appeared on bottles.

Victor Moët had no sons, so at the dawn of the twentieth century it was Raoul and Gaston Chandon de Briailles, Pierre-Gabriel's grandsons, who took over the business. Their father, Paul, had been ennobled in 1854 with the title of comte Chandon de Briailles. The two brothers, followed by their younger sibling Jean-Remy Chandon Moët (who obtained the right to adopt the name), consolidated the company's success through the Roaring Twenties. In 1930, the Chandon Moët family called upon another relative to run the business, Robert-Jean de Vogüé (whose wife inherited Victor Moët's property). Assisted in this task by the main shareholder, Frédéric Chandon de Briailles, de Vogüé remained in charge right up to 1972. As a refined aristocrat with an exceptional sense of business and social relations, he carried Moët & Chandon's glory to its height, even as he played a key role in the region's winemaking institutions: in 1941 he actively participated in the founding of the Comité Interprofessionnel du Vin de Champagne, which regulated the overall functioning of the wine economy. At Moët & Chandon, he instituted paid vacations and flexible working hours even before French legislation required them. As a member of the French Resistance during World War II, he was

arrested and deported to Germany in the company of the firm's main union organizer. It was the two men's friendship in the face of hardship that led to Moët & Chandon's exemplary employer–staff relationship. De Vogüé always functioned as a man ahead of his times, whose efforts left their mark on the history of champagne. In 1940 he relaunched the Moët Quarter, known as a "split," whose totally original size was a spectacular hit. In the late 1950s, he was the first champagne producer to set up subsidiaries abroad, the better to monitor his dealers and the company's image. As a friend of aristocrats and stars, he lent a new dimension to public relations. At the same time he promoted bold financial and industrial policies, typical of a visionary who mobilizes the resources to achieve that vision: he planted vineyards for the production of sparkling wine in Argentina; he listed Moët & Chandon on the stock market in 1962; he engineered a powerful luxury-goods corporation by buying not only champagne-makers Ruinart and Mercier, but also a stake in Dior perfumes; finally, he was the man who facilitated the merger with Hennessy in 1971.

IMPERIAL GENEROSITY

Today LVMH and Moët Hennessy own nearly 4,600 acres of vineyards in Champagne. Of this total, nearly 3,200 acres belong to Moët & Chandon, yet those vineyards produce only part of the grapes that go into the composition of Moët & Chandon's champagnes. The rest are bought from other winegrowers in Champagne. After every harvest, eight hundred different wines are submitted for the appreciation of the cellar master, Benoît Gouez, and his team of ten oenologists. Those that display the right qualities contribute to the "Moët & Chandon

FACING PAGE: *Grape picking in the 1930s. Large wicker baskets typical of the Champagne region (known as* mannequins*) were loaded on to carts that carried the grapes to the press after they had already been sorted on wicker trays by the women seen picking in the background.*

style," recognizable for its striking fruitiness, rich palate, and elegant maturity. Between one hundred and one hundred and fifty of these wines, made from the three varieties of Champagne grape, are included in Moët & Chandon Impérial, that great, classic French champagne enjoyed all over the world. This itself sums up the strange paradox of Moët & Chandon: the quantity and variety of the wines it uses in its blends are not only essential to the amount of champagne the company delivers, but are also the source of its reliable quality. This is because the more wines available when composing a given champagne, the easier it is for a cellar master to produce exactly what is desired, with no variation from year to year. Thus every year Moët & Chandon Impérial displays the same vibrant and generous qualities. Smooth and long in the mouth, Moët & Chandon Impérial is appreciated for its elegance, its balance, and its reliability, making it perfect for all occasions. Its fine effervescence, which lasts throughout the tasting from initial contact to the finish in the mouth, is one of its miracles, a secret product of ancestral skills at Moët & Chandon, now headed by Stéphane Baschiera. This legendary smoothness can also be appreciated in a champagne convincingly relaunched in 1996, Moët & Chandon Rosé Impérial, a lively yet silky wine with a fine cherry color displaying coppery highlights, and a fresh, fruity flavor evocative of wild strawberries. Such a spontaneous and appealing champagne reflects the glamorous side of the Moët & Chandon style.

The Impérial range, meanwhile, includes Nectar Impérial, an exotic, rich champagne, smooth yet with lively notes of fruit and honey. In 2010 Moët & Chandon launched Moët & Chandon Ice Impérial, specially designed to be enjoyed with ice. The idea was to develop a summer champagne whose balance and fruitiness would not be diluted, as would a standard champagne, by the addition of ice cubes.

The answer was to boost aromatic potential through a specific assemblage that exploited the intense fruitiness of Pinot Noir grapes, the richness of Pinot Meunier grapes, and the acidity of Chardonnay grapes. When well chilled, Moët & Chandon Ice Impérial reveals its aromatic intensity and rich fruity flavor balanced by and hint of acidity—it is perfect with a few leaves of mint, a zest of lemon, or even a touch of ginger.

Jean-Remy Moët had the chance to welcome important visitors to his town who then became his customers, including the Emperor Napoleon.

Every year, at grape-picking time, around September, Moët & Chandon's oenologists must confront the same issue: will there be enough high-quality grapes to yield a vintage champagne, in addition to the steadfast Moët & Chandon Impérial? Moët & Chandon refuses to attempt a vintage champagne every year, that is to say a blend made exclusively from the grapes of a single year. It is only during "assemblage," or blending, after the initial fermentation, that a decision will be taken. It would always be affirmative if the company agreed to set aside all of the year's best wines, but that would mean sacrificing the quality of Moët & Chandon Impérial which, as the flagship of the maker's reputation, is sacrosanct for Moët & Chandon. Hence vintage champagnes are only produced in the best years. The blending of a vintage champagne is all the trickier in that the cellar master, freed from the requirement of annual consistency, enjoys greater liberty in blending, and this can lead to intense debate within the team. Once the final assemblage is decided and completed, the champagne will be aged for five to seven years

FACING PAGE: *The château of Saran, purchased in the nineteenth century, is located on a Côte des Blancs estate where Chardonnay grapes reign supreme (top). Originally the residence of the Moët-Romont family, the château has played host to distinguished visitors since the 1950s. When blended with Pinot Noir and Pinot Meunier grapes, Chardonnay adds a touch of lightness (bottom, left). A late nineteenth-century portrait of Gaston Chandon de Brialles' elegant American wife, Mary Noey Re Tallack Garrisson, whom he met while promoting Moët & Chandon in the United States (bottom, right).*
PAGES 28–29: *The orangery provides a counterpoint to the buildings designed during the Empire period. Facing the orangery on the other side of the reflecting pool are the residential pavilions, one of which is the Trianon.*

before it is put on the market (the legal minimum is just three years). The quality of a Moët & Chandon Grand Vintage champagne is a function of time. At Moët & Chandon, the white and rosé vintage wines are magical, always full of delightful surprises. Complex and solid, these mature wines can be a perfect accompaniment to a meal assuming you are attentive to what they have to offer.

Vintage champagnes nevertheless faithfully reflect Moët & Chandon's own heritage through their strong personalities and obviously unique assemblages. Such continuity is demonstrated through the "Grand Vintage Collection": when each new Moët & Chandon Grand Vintage is marketed, it is henceforth accompanied by older vintages that form a coherent, harmonious ensemble. For example, the exceptional Moët & Chandon Grand Vintage 2002—marketed in 2010 after seven years of aging (a period not matched since 1930)—with its velvety texture and aromas of grains, frangipane, white peach, and nectarine, reveals its full palette of sensations in a comparative tasting of the related vintages of 1992, 1982, 1975, and 1964.

It is usually at Épernay that such extraordinary tastings are held in one of Moët & Chandon's two elegant pavilions. Whereas the hôtel Chandon was entirely revamped in the 1990s to provide meeting rooms, the other pavilion, the Trianon, receives distinguished guests in its lavishly authentic, and now meticulously restored, setting. Richard Wagner also appreciated the hospitality there during a stay in 1858, at the invitation of Paul Chandon de Briailles, who was an admirer of the great German composer. The residence still boasts an elegant music room among its various salons and halls, all magnificently decorated and furnished, most overlooking the wonderful garden with orangery. The nerve centers of the Trianon nevertheless remain the large dining room (with its hidden service passages) and the kitchen. Indeed, the

dining room is the throne room: at the Moët & Chandon table, it is champagne that reigns, and everything must bow to it. The task of the chef, Bernard Dance, in close collaboration with cellar master Gouez, is to bring out all the values of Moët & Chandon champagne. There the art of cuisine is geared toward creating refined dishes that will not overwhelm the champagne, and which champagne will enhance, in turn. This requires not only balance, but boldness. Since the Trianon frequently hosts enlightened connoisseurs and wine-industry professionals, vintage wines are often given pride of place. These champagnes have strong, powerful personalities, so they delight in bold combinations. The flavors of game, spices, mushrooms, truffles, caramel, and chocolate are studied at length, then carefully prepared, in the goal of bringing out the unique qualities of a Moët & Chandon Grand Vintage. For a bottle of vintage 1983, for example, the chef devised a dish of poultry with licorice root for the champagne's notes of wood and sweet spices; the 1990 rosé, meanwhile, calls for foie gras with berries and spice.

This refined quest for the finest combinations of food and champagne is not limited to the company chef. On the contrary, the aim is to expand horizons, to inspire—and be inspired by—masters of other national cuisines. The release of Grand Vintages, which trigger tastings around the world accompanied by meals devised by great local chefs, represent splendid occasions for this quest.

The Trianon, across from the orangery, receives distinguished guests in its lavishly authentic, and now meticulously restored, setting.

FACING PAGE: *Details of the entrance to the lavish residence where Jean-Remy Moët received Napoleon whenever the emperor passed through Épernay. The first visit followed Napoleon's successful negotiation of the treaty of Tilsitt in 1807. As a great champagne lover, the emperor always had supplies on hand, even on the battlefield. In a tribute to its famous guest, Moët & Chandon registered the "Impérial" label for its fine champagnes in 1863. The Trianon is still used today to host the company's distinguished visitors.*
PAGE 33: *A few bottles stashed away in Moët & Chandon's cellars serve as a reminder that the cellar master's creative talent blossoms within traditional practices in which time plays an important role.*

You might think that makers of champagne always repeat
the same thing, that there's no creativity. But the range of soils,
years, grape varieties, and experience generates an unsuspected diversity
within the Champagne region. Each house structures its range
differently, between vintages and non-vintage Bruts.
The Moët & Chandon Impérial is a compulsory figure,
fully controlled—we know exactly where we're headed, it's a rational job
carried out by a team. In contrast, the Grand Vintage is free style—a
unique creation, a one-off interpretation that has its own attributes.
It gives greater freedom to the cellar master,
who tries to give expression to everything that goes into the vintage
in question, taking in account supplies, vineyards, harvest, taste
impression, grape varieties, and so on. He can be more creative,
interpreting the house style in a personal way, making a mark.

Benoît Gouez
CELLAR MASTER

Tasting notes

VINTAGE: Grand Vintage 2002
HARVEST: Combined effect of wind and hot, dry weather concentrated the juices; very even ripening across
the various grape varieties and villages.
ASSEMBLAGE: 51 percent Chardonnay — 26 percent Pinot Noir — 23 percent Pinot Meunier.
DOSAGE: 5.5 grams per liter
FIRST NOSE: Aromas of frangipani, grilled almonds and malt, mocha and light tobacco, evolving toward
notes of pear, candied citrus fruit, and stone fruits.
ATTACK IN MOUTH: Round and creamy; concludes with a lively, refreshing finale.
PERFECT COMBINATIONS: Sea urchins, scallops, king prawns, and wild salmon.

Such was the case in 2008, for example, when the exceptional Moët & Chandon Grand Vintage 2003 was presented. That year, the vineyards had experienced totally unprecedented climate conditions: a winter-long frost lasted into April, a hailstorm hit in spring, and then August featured a heat wave that brought the harvest forward to August 18, the earliest date in 181 years. Such an atypical harvest would inevitably produce an atypical wine. After weeks of anxiety, the verdict fell: 2003 would yield a unique wine. Five years later, the mature champagne featured initial tastes of vanilla and almond followed by impressions of sun-drenched fruit, soon joined by hints of spice. Such a profound, generous wine could be further magnified by a meal comprised of dense, strongly flavored dishes. Grand Vintage 2003 thus began its world tour accompanied by four other vintages in a Grand Vintage Collection (1995, 1990, 1976, and 1959) that allowed for revelatory comparative tastings. Certain stages of this tour were as bold as they were successful. The great chef at the Casino de Madrid, Paco Roncero, a specialist in Spanish "mini-portion cuisine," suggested enhancing the 2003 with olive-oil butter alone, a perfect marriage of creamy textures that combined sweetness and bitterness. Meanwhile, Albert Wong, the chef at Sevva in Hong Kong, exalted the wine's fruitiness by serving roasted pigeon with grapefruit and tangerine sauce (at Épernay, Bernard Dance adopted the same approach with lobster poached in Moët & Chandon accompanied by mango mousse). In the two-star restaurant named after him, Milan chef Claudio Sadler underscored the generosity of Grand Vintage 2003 through varied textures and delicate contrasts between hints of iodine, acidity, and fruit by serving sea urchins with cauliflower cream, marinated salmon, and raspberry vinegar. It is probably no coincidence that this same Grand Vintage was inspiration for a similar combination with sea urchins

Between one hundred and one hundred and fifty wines, made from the three varieties of Champagne grape are included in Moët & Chandon Impérial, that great, classic French champagne enjoyed all over the world.

at the Ryugin restaurant in Tokyo, where chef Seiji Yamamoto has also earned two Michelin stars. Loyal to traditional *kaiseki* cuisine, Yamamoto came up with a firework display of three flavors and three textures that explode in the mouth simultaneously: a premium sea urchin wrapped in dry seaweed and fried with buckwheat flour. During this same meal, still designed to illustrate the Grand Vintage 2003, the Japanese chef pursued his triple approach with a fascinating little dish of three types of textures of abalone with cold vegetables and scallop jelly.

Toward the close of the first decade of the new millennium, Moët & Chandon decided it was important to encourage its loyal fans to adopt an innovative approach to combinations of food and wine. It therefore organized champagne-based culinary workshops all around the world. Following a launch in France, the first workshops were held in Italy, Belgium, Australia, the United States, and China. This time, starting with a tasting of a Moët & Chandon Grand Vintage 2002, the participants—composed of chefs, wine stewards, and specialized journalists—were invited to choose the ingredients themselves. They selected the produce and seasonings best adapted to the richness of wine, working with the Moët & Chandon chef to create one or several simple dishes.

FACING PAGE: *A view of a tiny section of the seventeen miles of cellars, still owned by Moët & Chandon today, cut from fossil-studded limestone. They form a maze beneath the streets of Épernay.*
PAGE 36: *The tricky moment of riddling has arrived for bottles that have aged sufficiently, according to the cellar master. They rest on tilted racks, waiting for the riddler to give them a slight turn—first right, then left (they are regularly turned, or riddled, over a period of four to six weeks to encourage yeast deposits to slide gently toward the neck of the bottle). Some fifty to fifty-two thousand bottles are riddled every day in Moët & Chandon's cellars.*
PAGE 37: *Elsewhere in the cellars, older bottles patiently wait to be tasted.*

Discussion, preparation, and tasting enabled the participants to refine their perception of the champagne, the better to discover and understand it qualities, which were then highlighted by new recipes.

Another educational experience is proposed to foreign chefs at demonstrations performed all over the world: three Moët & Chandon champagnes are placed beside a very straightforward, basic food (say white meat, shrimp, or scallops) plus a few ingredients used to accompany it in succession— salt, lemon, soy sauce, olive oil, ginger, honey, etc. As the tasting session progresses from salty to bitter and from acidic to sweet, perception of the wines is transformed. This exercise enables the chefs present to appreciate the potential of champagne all the better, in order to allow it to resonate with recipes from their own culinary culture. In this case the tasting is done with three different champagnes, three variations on the Moët & Chandon style, so that the chefs can multiply the range of possibilities and pleasures.

Sweet dishes are alleged to be the enemies of champagne, but that is not the case with a vintage 1962, which was recently brought up from the cellar for a classic tasting session among a few select connoisseurs. The year 1962 was an exceptional vintage, with notes of toasted brioche, raisins, and caramel. It was also a key element— blended with an assemblage of other great vintage years from the century—in a special new millennium-celebration wine, creating a most exceptional champagne dubbed "Esprit du Siècle"

At Moët & Chandon, the white and rosé vintage wines are always full of delightful surprises.

[Spirit of the Century] which was produced in only 323 magnums. On the day of this particular tasting, the 1962 was served with dessert, namely pineapple candied in spiced caramel. "Sweet yet sharp," explained the chef, "the power of the spices, softened by the caramel and underscored by the acidity of the pineapple, creates a perfect harmony with this nectar."

Today the aristocratic splendor of Moët & Chandon sparkles in one hundred and fifty countries around the world, thanks above all to the quality of its wine yet perhaps also because of the firm's long-running, close relationship to the world of movies. Ever since 1952, the year when Moët & Chandon was first sipped by the stars at the Cannes International Film Festival, the company has been associated with the film industry's most glamorous events. They range from major festivals in San Sebastian, Locarno, Venice, Toronto to the two top-tier international events: the Golden Globe Awards (where Moët & Chandon is drunk at the gala dinner) and the Oscars (for which Moët & Chandon has been the exclusive supplier since 2009). During these festivities, celebrities are invited to sign large-sized bottles—jeroboams and over—which are then sold at auction to the benefit of charity organizations.

FACING PAGE: *The architecture of the company's storage cellars is now part of the town of Épernay's historic heritage (top). Throughout the year, the Trianon remains faithful to its calling by hosting Moët & Chandon's distinguished guests in a lavish nineteenth-century decor (bottom).*
PAGE 41: *Chef Bernard Dance invents dishes designed to underscore the personality of the company's champagnes. His recipes emerge from an ongoing exchange with cellar master Benoît Gouez, and are then shared with star chefs from all over the world, who are great connoisseurs of Moët & Chandon champagne.*

CUCUMBER EMULSION WITH FRESH MINT, SEARED SCALLOPS, ORANGE GASTRIQUE, AND CUCUMBER BEADS WITH BLACK PEPPER

INGREDIENTS

Serves 4

Orange Gastrique:
· ½ cup plus 2 tablespoons (150 ml) wine vinegar
· ½ cup (3 ½ oz./100 g) sugar
· Juice of ½ orange

Cucumber Beads:
· 1 large cucumber
· 1 tablespoon (15 g) butter
· Freshly ground black pepper

· A few mint leaves, finely chopped
· 12 scallops
· A little olive oil
· Fleur de sel

METHOD

Orange Gastrique: Prepare a light caramel with the vinegar and sugar. Add the orange juice and reduce until the sauce thickens. Keep warm.

Cucumber Beads: Peel the cucumber. With a small scoop, shape the cucumber beads. Set aside the trimmings to use for the emulsion. Melt the butter in a pan. When it sizzles, add the cucumbers and cook for 1 minute. Season with freshly ground black pepper.

Cucumber Emulsion: Remove the seeds from the cucumber trimmings and cut into small pieces. Place them in the food processor and add a little water and salt. Process until smooth. Pour into a small bowl and add the chopped mint. Immediately place in the refrigerator.

Scallops: Season the scallops with salt and pepper and sauté them for a few minutes in a pan with a little olive oil. Remove from the heat.

To Plate: In a deep dish, spoon out the well-chilled cucumber emulsion. Arrange the hot scallops in a triangle and drizzle with the orange gastrique. Scatter the hot cucumber beads on each side of the scallops. Sprinkle fleur de sel over the orange gastrique.

FOR A BOTTLE OF VINTAGE 1983, THE CHEF DEVISED A DISH OF POULTRY WITH LICORICE ROOT FOR THE CHAMPAGNE'S NOTES OF WOOD AND SWEET SPICES; THE 1990 ROSÉ, MEANWHILE, CALLS FOR FOIE GRAS WITH BERRIES AND SPICE.

ABOVE: *To do justice to the Grand Vintage white and rosé champagnes, the cellar master and his team of experts designed a special flute glass perfectly suited to tasting them (left). Chef Bernard Dance is master of the house at the Trianon (right).*
FACING PAGE: *In the dining room with its elegant white eighteenth-century woodwork and windows overlooking the orangery, the table is set with silver and china for a dinner at which a few special guests will enjoy the elegant experience of a traditional French meal.*

Champagne

MERCIER

Champagne

As the founder of one of the most democratic champagnes, Eugène Mercier would be delighted to learn that his cellars, one hundred and thirty years after they were built, are still included in travel guides from around the world. Until recently the majestic Orient Express from Paris shunted onto a special siding at Épernay where it slowly rolled straight to the private platform of the house of Mercier. There, several dozen tourists descended from the art-deco train carriages (listed as historical monuments) and followed a red carpet, only a few yards long, which led them without having to descend a single stair, straight to wine cellars in which fifteen thousand bottles were patiently waiting. Because what the Orient Express passengers experienced, just by crossing the width of a train platform, is one very concrete example of Mercier's extraordinary goal: to make champagne more accessible to all. And the railroad was a modern invention that put champagne within the reach of all, in more senses than one, as it increased the number of bottles sold and subsequently lowered retail prices. Eugène Mercier devoted his entire life to this generous idea, which was truly revolutionary in the days when champagne was still reserved for an elite.

This vision may well have been due to Mercier's humble background. Born in 1838, his mother was a modest shopkeeper in Épernay. She became a mother in her teenage years, and Eugène never knew his father. After a brief education in a Catholic school, at age thirteen he was hired by a winegrower from Cramant, while at sixteen he apparently became an errand boy for a notary. Little is known of these years of apprenticeship, but we do know that by age twenty, Eugène was a gifted and ambitious young man, if poor. As he strolled down the broad boulevard then known as Faubourg de la Folie (today's Avenue de Champagne), already flanked by the magnificent homes of the major champagne dynasties, he must have thought how he'd like to have his own home there one day. But how? The answer he came up with, at the age of twenty, reveals his budding genius. With his own modest savings and those of his mother, he founded the Union des Propriétaires, a federation of small champagne-makers whose wines he would market himself. The principle behind this idea was one that guided his entire life: to sell as cheaply as possible. Not by stinting on quality, but by lowering the cost price by all

COMPAGNIE DES GRANDS VINS DE CHAMPAGNE
UNION DE PROPRIÉTAIRES
FONDÉE EN 1858
E. MERCIER & Cᵒ
CHATEAU DE PÉKIN (ÉPERNAY)
PRODUCTION ANNUELLE MOYENNE DEUX MILLIONS DE BOUTEILLES DE CHAMPAGNE
DIPLÔME D'HONNEUR
DIPLÔME D'HONNEUR A ROCHEFORT

possible means. The first stage was this union of small winemakers, allowing them to share marketing costs. By the end of the nineteenth century, some forty champagne houses had joined, and Mercier was also selling champagne aged in his own cellars, under his own name.

The idea of such a federation was new, and it got off to a shaky start. But it steadily built up a solid clientele, including some glamorous champagne merchants worried about finding themselves short on supplies and impressed by the quality of its products. Less then ten years after founding his business, Mercier found his premises cramped and, at last disposing of some capital, decided to implement the second stage of his cost-cutting plan: to dig vast, functional cellars. The year was 1869, and the Paris-to-Strasbourg railroad had already been running through Épernay for seventeen years. The track ran along the foot of a hill some one hundred feet high, Le Bernon, up which the Faubourg de la Folie headed in the direction of Châlons. Eugène Mercier immediately recognized all the advantages of this blessed site: the glamorous address, the proximity of rail transportation, and the possibility of digging caves straight into the chalky hill at the same level as the train tracks. So he bought a large plot of land on the hill.

As soon as the Franco-Prussian war of 1870 had ended, work began on the cellars. Mercier tore up the standard blueprints proposed by his architects, who had envisaged several levels of cellars, and instructed them to design the space on a single level—that of the train tracks. "Think in terms of miles!" he explained. He wound up with eleven miles of galleries, dug by hand with picks and shovels, laid out as a simple grid. The work lasted for nearly six years, during which Mercier acquired many nearby plots of land. He used the chalk extracted from the cellars to embank part of the bed of the Marne River, making it easier to lay the half-mile of private track he would need. He also used this same chalk to build the platform.

In 1877, the Mercier firm became the first champagne house to ship its champagne by train. The boxcar could be parked just in front of his cellars, from which emerged horse carts laden with cases. Considerable savings were made in relation to conventional shipping costs.

Mercier's gigantic facilities, easily visible from the station in Épernay where trains halted to take on coal, were the firm's first free advertising coup. Eugène then began to develop another of his revolutionary ideas, later imitated by thousands of winemakers and wine dealers: he organized tours of his wine cellar. The first tour took place in 1875, even before work was completed. Over time, the tours became more and more sophisticated. Mercier had sculptor Gustave André Navlet decorate his cellars with high-relief carvings still visible today. Staff were specially trained to welcome visitors by 1885, and the following year, in another world-first, the cellars were lit by electricity. This tradition has been unflaggingly

To put champagne within the reach of all, Eugène Mercier devoted his entire life to this generous idea, which was truly revolutionary in the days when champagne was still reserved for an elite.

respected and perfected; with over one hundred and forty thousand visitors per year, Mercier is by far the leading champagne house in this field.

Costs had to be lowered further still. For Eugène Mercier that meant supplying the market with a great quantity of wine that was reliably uniform in quality. But the barrels then being used for blending, which contained between one hundred and fifty to two hundred and fifty gallons, didn't allow for this possibility.

FACING PAGE: *The blending cellar in the early twentieth century (top). The blending operation was formerly done with casks of six hundred to one thousand liters (roughly one hundred and fifty to two hundred and fifty gallons), but today is done in glass-lined concrete vats. A display of various medals won by Mercier champagnes when competing at International Expositions (bottom, left). A portrait of the company founder, Eugène Mercier (1838–1904), toward the end of his life (bottom, right). This visionary entrepreneur built an empire on a simple idea that was revolutionary at the time: make champagne more easily accessible to all.*

So even as his cellars were being dug, Mercier decided to commission a cooper in Nancy to make a giant barrel. He wanted a barrel that could contain the equivalent of no fewer than seventy-five thousand bottles, which was unheard of at the time. But Mercier didn't stop there. At about the same time he asked another cooper to design a tun that could hold two hundred thousand bottles, that is to say forty-two thousand gallons! One hundred and fifty oak trees, to be felled in Hungary, would be required to make this cask. Lumberjacks began their work in 1872 but the tun wasn't completed until 1885. Like the cellars, this modern production tool was soon turned into a tool of advertising. Mercier decided to display his tun—decorated by Navlet with a monumental relief showing an allegory of Champagne offering a bunch of grapes to England—at the 1889 Universal Exhibition in Paris. The gigantic cask weighed twenty tons, and had to be pulled from Épernay to Paris by twelve pairs of oxen. During the entire week-long journey, an enormous crowd, whipped up by the press, lined up to watch the procession pass. Trees and sometimes even walls had to be brought down to make room—even the entrance to the exhibition had to be widened. Mercier's huge cask was the star of the show, along with Eiffel's huge tower.

A true pioneer of modern publicity, Mercier continued to dream up extraordinary events. During the Universal Exhibition of 1900, a tethered hot-air balloon decorated with the words "Champagne Mercier" lifted a total of ten thousand visitors, twelve at a time, some one thousand feet above Paris. Eugène Mercier died in 1904. His heirs have pursued the same policy of innovation in all fields, respecting the brand's identity as an excellent but affordable champagne. Jacques Mercier, Eugène's grandson, headed the firm from the 1950s to the 1970s and was the first champagne maker to take an interest in the emerging supermarket chains. He was also the first to use stainless steel vats for better control over fermentation. Mercier became the most widely drunk champagne in France. Yet ever aware of the vulnerability of a lone brand in an increasingly competitive market, Jacques Mercier accepted Moët & Chandon's offer of a merger in 1970. By combining their strengths and their production facilities the two neighboring houses were able to considerably reinforce one another.

THE PLEASURE OF COMPANY

The best-loved champagne in France, Mercier should be drunk with simplicity and conviviality, as its founder intended. Its wines are noted for their refreshing spontaneity and pleasantly fruity notes. Of course, there is nothing more complicated than obtaining this impression of spontaneity and natural freshness from a living, fermented, product. The firm's team of winemakers nevertheless manage to do so each year, come what may, working from six or seven hundred different wines. The colossal task of tasting, blending, and aging results in a range of six types of champagne now marketed by Mercier. The brut, or dry, version is perfect as an aperitif, given its gentle attack and its refreshing hint of citrus fruit, which it owes to an assemblage based primarily on Pinot Noir and Pinot Meunier grapes. The same gentle attack and intense freshness can be found in the Brut Rosé, composed exclusively of Pinot grapes, largely Pinot Noir, to give it that characteristic taste of red fruit, making it ideal for the table as well as an aperitif. Mercier's oenologists also compose two other dry champagnes. Cuvée Eugène Mercier is an assemblage with a high proportion of reserve wines, which lend maturity and roundness to its bouquet of cooked apple and caramel, and make it sturdy enough to be drunk throughout a meal.

PAGES 50–51: *The delicate process of riddling. Once the ageing period has come to an end, the bottles are placed in tilted racks, awaiting a gentle rotation. Every day for a six-to eight-week period the riddler gives the bottle a 45-degree turn. The point is to urge the yeast deposits that have formed to slide gently to the neck of the bottle. Today riddling is largely done on motorized racks, called gyropalettes, able to handle a larger number of bottles.*
FACING PAGE: *As an early advertising strategist, the founder made his company known to the general public. Here, in 1900, a balloon flight sponsored by Mercier linked Paris to Épernay—the successful flight was widely reported in the press. As early as 1898 Mercier commissioned the company's first advertising film from the Lumière brothers, the French movie pioneers.*

At Mercier, the vintage champagne expresses our house image.
But we only produce it in small quantities. We feel we're always able
to select the finest batches every year to *make* a vintage wine, but only
later do we decide whether or not to market it, taking both qualitative
and commercial considerations into account. In 2001 we made a
vintage champagne but didn't market it. Whereas with our Brut
champagne we can reproduce the same style every year by using a range
of materials, with the vintage we try to interpret or illustrate a specific
year. It's the expression of a unique perception, a record of that year.
Mercier makes fruity, fresh champagnes to be enjoyed by everyone—its
DNA contains the generous spirit of the founder, Eugène Mercier.
Mercier's vintage champagne is somewhat paradoxical,
because it's young. Somewhat nonconformist.

———————

Christophe Bonnefond
CELLAR MASTER

Tasting notes

VINTAGE: 2007
HARVEST: A varied summer, but a healthy vineyard resulted in early ripening; picking in the last days of August
was a sign of quality and quantity. Good sun during harvest; selective picking, along with adjustments to normal
picking patterns, allowed for a highly qualitative choice of grapes from an uneven harvest.
ASSEMBLAGE: 39 percent Chardonnay — 31 percent Pinot Noir — 30 percent Pinot Meunier.
DOSAGE: 8 to 9 grams per liter
FIRST NOSE: Notes of peach, nectarine, and pears evolving toward hints of brioche.
ATTACK IN MOUTH: Full and generous, structured around notes of fruit and spices right to the end.
PERFECT COMBINATIONS: Ideal as an aperitif; at dinner, goes with foie gras and white fish such turbot,
sea bass, and monkfish.

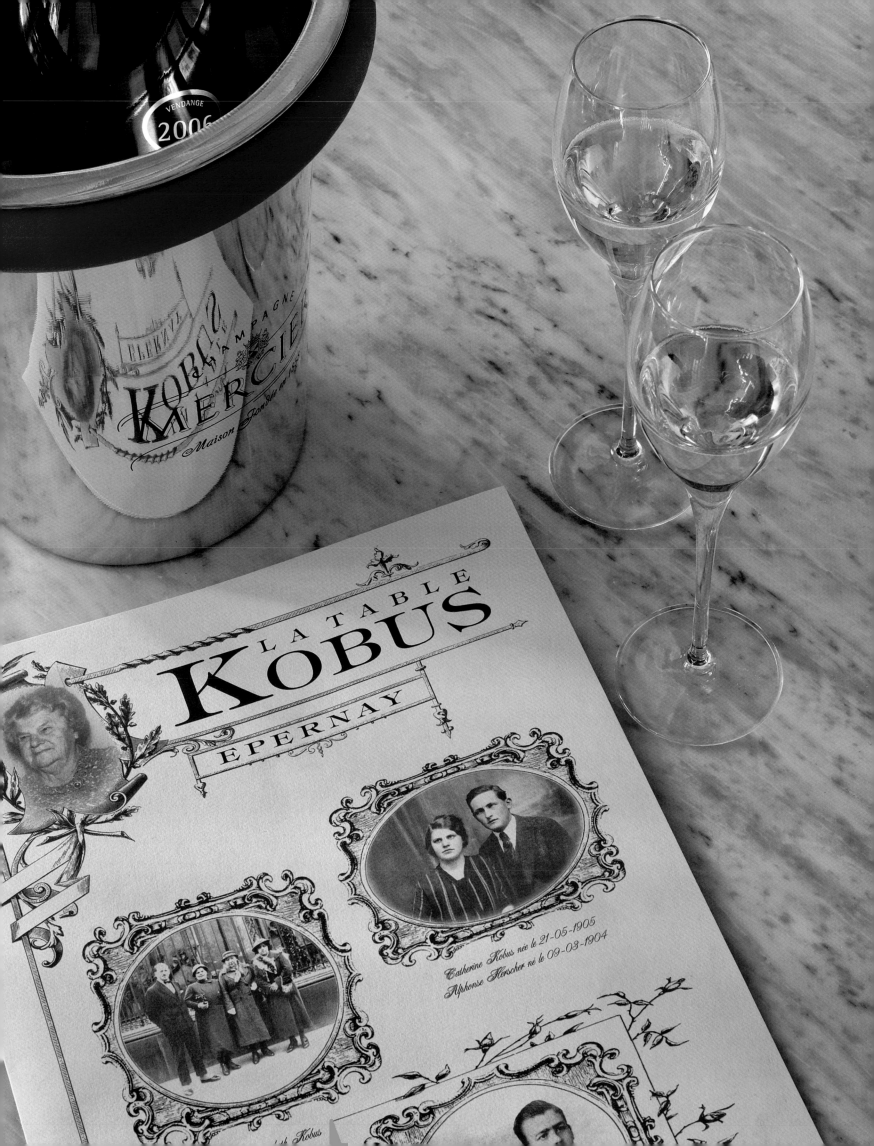

Catherine Kobus née le 21-05-1905
Alphonse Herscher né le 09-03-1904

The other dry Mercier is a vintage champagne, called Vendange (followed by the year). Mercier produces a vintage wine every year; whatever the general characteristics of the harvest, Mercier manages to find enough high-quality grapes to make a marketable quantity of vintage bottles. Like all Mercier champagnes, although richer and more complex, Vendange is characterized by a gentle, fresh taste with a certain intensity. Finally, Mercier offers two "demi-sec," or sweet, champagnes, that bring a rich hint of honey and dried fruit to the palate, and are recommended primarily to accompany desserts but go equally well with foie gras, certain sweet-and-savory dishes, and a few strong cheeses such as blue cheese made from cow's milk. Like all Mercier champagnes, the demi-secs remain lively and fresh in the mouth. Demi-Sec Rosé—the firm's most recent champagne—offers a further touch of exotic fruit that works wonders, for example, with the spicy cuisine of the Near East and Asia. From time to time Mercier seeks out the talent of a young chef such as Guillaume Bachellez of the *Table Kobus* restaurant in Épernay to devise straightforward dishes—never combining more than three flavors—that give full scope to the fresh attack and fruity intensity of the Cuvée Eugène Mercier.

All of Mercier's champagnes are known for their brilliant, luminous color, which prefigures the intense sensations experienced in their nose and palate. They are sunny wines that speak of holidays, get-aways, and simple pleasures shared in a casual, friendly way. The Mercier premises on Avenue de la Champagne (as it is now called) were entirely renovated in 1989 to reflect the wines themselves: bold, dynamic, intense. Light pours in through a glass roof and gilds the pale wood of the giant cask that greets visitors. A panoramic elevator allows the same visitors to reach the cellars, one hundred feet below, at a stately pace. During the descent, pictures of tasks related to the vineyards and vinification, carved into the chalk, pass by. Then a small, laser-guided train, the successor to the electric train first installed in 1952, takes visitors on a tour of the cellar. Mercier has always liked being open to the public, and it devotes considerable resources to this tour, proving itself worthy of the founder's legendary generosity. Only certain special visitors, however, get to see, on certain evenings, the Cave of Bacchus: a magnificent door in the form of a cask opens onto a large vaulted hall, the former disgorging cellar now transformed into a reception room.

The best-loved champagne in France, Mercier should be drunk with simplicity and conviviality, as its founder intended.

The room hosts groups for events including gourmet meals savored with Mercier's finest champagnes. The hall is decorated with two vast reliefs carved by Navlet, including the allegorical figure, originally sculpted there in 1881, reproduced on the giant tun. Further along, in a private zone reserved for Mercier's own oenologists, is the "Oenethèque," or vintage cellar. It occupies a former chalk pit, the "Glacière" or "Ice House," because Eugène Mercier, never short on ideas, originally used it to store blocks of ice cut from the frozen Marne River in winter, which he would then sell to local restaurant owners in the spring and summer. This cellar, with its ideal constant temperature of 12°C (54°F), far from the bustle of the main cellars, is home to dozens of old bottles of vintage champagne, most of them not yet disgorged, waiting patiently to deliver their promises. The oldest bottle dates back to 1923.

PAGE 55: *"Mercier's vintage champagne is paradoxical, because it is young," the cellar master likes to say. And its youth makes it a wine to be shared in all simplicity with everyone, everywhere.*
FACING PAGE: *The company's "oenothèque," or vintage cellar, houses the oldest champagnes in a small limestone cave (top). Only special guests are admitted to this sanctuary. Cellar master Christophe Bonnefond tastes wines after the harvest in order to identify the aromatic qualities of each batch (bottom, left). Only then will he determine the blend that creates the Mercier style, known for its intense notes of fruit. The decoration of the cellars represents a tribute to the vine and winemakers (bottom, right).*

ROASTED LINE-CAUGHT SEA BASS,
POIVRADE ARTICHOKES IN *JUS*, AND CHAMPAGNE SAUCE

INGREDIENTS

Serves 4

· 12 poivrade artichokes
· Juice of 1 lemon
· 1 onion, chopped
· Scant ½ cup (100 ml) olive oil
· 1 cup (250 ml) white wine
· 2 cups (500 ml) white chicken stock
· 4 fillets sea bass, each about 6 oz.
  (180 g)
· Salt and pepper

Champagne Sauce:
· 3 ½ oz. (100 g) shallots, chopped
· 1 sprig thyme
· 1 cup (250 ml) white wine
· 2 cups (500 ml) fish fumet
· 1 cup (250 ml) heavy cream
· ¾ cup (200 ml) champagne Brut
· Salt and pepper

· Chervil leaves and beet shoots for
  garnish

METHOD

Trim the poivrade artichokes, making sure to retain their shape. Dip them in water with lemon juice so that they do not darken. Sauté them briefly with the chopped onion in a little olive oil. Season with salt and pepper. Deglaze with the white wine. Pour in the chicken stock and simmer for 10 minutes.

Make the champagne sauce: In a pot, sweat the chopped shallots with the thyme. Deglaze with the white wine and reduce. Add the fish fumet and reduce by half. Pour in the cream and then the champagne. Adjust the seasoning.

With a sharp knife, make incisions in the skin of the sea bass. Season with salt and pepper. Heat some olive oil in a skillet over high heat. Sear the fish fillets, skin side down, until nicely colored. Turn them over and finish cooking. Arrange the fillets and poivrade artichokes on a dish. Garnish with the chervil leaves and beet shoots. Serve the champagne sauce on the side.

Mercier possesses another priceless treasure, its museum of winepresses, which the public can visit during national "open days." Housed in a cellar that formerly served as pressing room, this unique collection boasts thirty-two presses ranging in date from the fourteenth to the nineteenth century. These large, impressive instruments of wood or metal retrace the history of wine pressing in Champagne from the days of still wines. There are also presses originally used in Alsace and Burgundy, and even a few cider presses from Normandy. The evolution of ancestral techniques is visible there, right up to the development of the early "industrial" winepresses. These latter testify not only to the ingenuity of winemakers but also their attachment to their tools, which they decorated with lively carved ornamentation. The winepress museum, like the first electric train in the cellars and the renovation of the Cave of Bacchus, was largely the work of Jean Couten, Eugène Mercier's great-grandson, who was general manager and then CEO of Mercier from 1970 to 1990. Couten traveled the length and breadth of France in search of these wonderful machines and meticulously restored them; all are in working condition. He collected them in this vast old cellar, following in the footsteps of his forebear Eugène, who decorated his cellars and casks with fine, sculpted frescoes. It is the aim of the house of Mercier to offer to the widest possible public not only champagne itself, but also the beauty and nobility of the art of making wine.

PAGE 59: *The lifestyle incarnated by Mercier champagne reflects authentic taste and simple pleasures.*
FACING PAGE: *A view of Le Train Bleu restaurant in the Gare-de-Lyon station in Paris. pIts legendary decor takes diners back to the wonderful era when "gay Paris" danced to the sound of champagne corks popping at every table—and when Eugène Mercier introduced his "Founders' Special Blend" at the Universal Exposition of 1900, held at the foot of the Eiffel Tower.*

Champagne

DOM PÉRIGNON

The first two words of the Rule of Saint Benedict are "Listen carefully." They are words that inevitably come to mind when visiting the abbey of Hautvillers on a hill overlooking the Marne Valley. Harvest period aside, silence reigns over the abbey, its vines, and its vast grounds, only gently disturbed by a light breeze in the tall cedars, by the sweet chirp of birds, or by the soft thud of a chestnut falling onto the carpet of dead leaves. In days of yore, by listening carefully you could also have detected the sound of the sparkling wine that Dom Pierre Pérignon was perfecting in his cellar. Even though the birth of champagne in the seventeenth century had many causes, it is impossible to overlook the connection between the invention of a divine wine, to which the soul is invited to hearken, and the monastic rule of Saint Benedict. The monks spent their entire lives listening attentively. Surely Dom Pierre Pérignon, so well trained in this spiritual exercise, must have sought to lend speech to his holy wine, and tasted it with his eyes closed.

Founded in the mid seventh century by Saint Nivard, the abbey of Hautvillers was a hospitable establishment located near the royal city of Reims. It enjoyed several heydays during a life spanning over a thousand years, notably thanks to the relics of Saint Helen (which came into its possession in the year 841), to its scriptorium (which was famous in the Middle Ages), and to the patronage of the Medici family in the sixteenth century. The abbey's fame spread even further thanks to one monk, Dom Pierre Pérignon, who arrived there in 1668, aged thirty, to assume the task of cellar master. He was also named procurator, that is to say he oversaw all the abbey's temporal affairs, and he held both offices for forty-seven years, which is most unusual among Benedictines. Dom Pierre's main job was to help the monastery prosper and to nurture its assets, chief among them being its vineyards. It was a crucial mission, because when he assumed office the abbey was a jumble of half-ruined buildings surrounded by neglected land due to a series of invasions and civil wars. In order to meet the needs of the religious community, to receive traveling nobles and pilgrims, and to take care of the poor, Hautvillers needed money. Right up to his death in 1715, Dom Pierre Pérignon worked in the spirit of the Benedictine rule of perfection that urged monks to take care in everything and to overlook nothing; he strived to revive the vineyards and he carried out research and experiments to make the wine from

PERIGNON 17
ER DE L'ABBAYE

the abbey of Hautvillers "the best in world," as he wrote in his own correspondence.

Producing the best wine in the world in order to secure sufficient income was certainly the creative monk's goal and even obsession. Thanks to his sense of observation, his innovative spirit, and his rigorous approach, Dom Pierre Pérignon refined and perfected vinification techniques, including making white wine from local red grapes, assembling wines from different vineyard plots, and pressing the "must" several times. His constantly innovative work was rewarded with success. Even during his lifetime the fame of "Dom Pérignon's wine" meant that it would sell for four times as much as its competitors, a fact which did not escape the attention of the merchants who supplied the royal household of King Louis XIV (Dom Pierre Pérignon's exact contemporary, as it transpired). During the subsequent regency, followed by the reign of Louis XV—that is to say, during the libertine and pleasure-seeking eighteenth century—the name Pérignon which d'Artagnan called the best *vin de champagne* was even assumed by some people to be the name of a specific vineyard.

Two centuries later, it was the discovery and adoption by wealthy connoisseurs on the other side of the Atlantic that really sealed this reputation, introducing champagne to the modern world of luxury products. On December 2, 1936, one hundred cases of vintage 1921 left France for America aboard the cruise liner *Normandie*. They were unloaded in New York just in time for Christmas and the New Year festivities. The champagne's instant success was a notable event that turned this vintage into a legendary year: nearly seventy years later, a lot of three bottles of Dom Pérignon 1921 was auctioned in London for nearly 25,000 dollars.

Thanks to his sense of observation, his innovative spirit, and his rigorous approach, Dom Pierre Pérignon refined and perfected vinification techniques, including making white wine from local red grapes, assembling wines from different vineyard plots, and pressing the "must" several times.

Down through the years the many devotees of Dom Pérignon champagne have been writing a kind of imaginary "visitor's book." If such a book actually existed, its signatures would include artists, filmmakers, actors, writers, and celebrities of the past and present centuries, all of whom recount, from their personal viewpoint full of quips, prosaic flourishes, and anecdotes, what brought them to Dom Pérignon. They would all have one thing in common: they are almost all creative men and women who wanted to transcend dogma, expand horizons, and forge new criteria. Such a book would include Truman Capote, the author of *Breakfast at Tiffany's*, for whom Dom Pérignon was the champagne par excellence, that no one could refuse, not even people "who don't like champagne." And it would include Orson Welles, one of whose great pleasures in life was sipping a glass or two of Dom Pérignon to accompany the prawn sandwiches served at Harry's Bar in Venice. Then there was Christian Dior, who never failed to offer a glass of Dom Pérignon to guests at his fine home in the Passy neighborhood of Paris (as he did

PAGES 66–67: *Saint Peter's abbey on the Dom Pérignon estate rises on the heights above the village of Hautvillers. The aesthetic purity and the spiritual heritage of the site are what allow privileged visitors to sense the "extra soul" that goes into Dom Pérignon vintage champagnes.*
FACING PAGE: *The abbey chapel features a carved portrait of Dom Pierre Pérignon, the monk who became the tutelary figure for all wine growers in Champagne. In the seventeenth century he was appointed estate manager there. He methodically studied winemaking in order to make the most of the abbey's vineyards, and he invented the sparkling wine that would one day be dubbed champagne.*

ON DECEMBER 2, 1936, ONE HUNDRED CASES
OF VINTAGE 1921 LEFT FRANCE FOR AMERICA
AND WERE UNLOADED IN NEW YORK.
THE CHAMPAGNE'S INSTANT SUCCESS
WAS A NOTABLE EVENT THAT TURNED
THIS VINTAGE INTO A LEGENDARY YEAR.

ABOVE AND FACING PAGE: *Dom Pierre Pérignon's tombstone in the chapel, the bell tower, and the buttresses*
of the cloister all recall the timeless presence of the Benedictine monks who founded Hautvillers in the seventh century
and who proved themselves to be the best winemakers in Champagne in the days of Dom Pierre Pérignon.

to Stanley Kernow, the famous *Time* correspondent who penned the first article on a fashion designer to make the cover of the popular news magazine). Some fifty years later, in 2005, it was the turn of another leading figure in the world of fashion and luxury, Karl Lagerfeld, who was to supervise the photo campaign to accompany the launching of Dom Pérignon's vintage 1998. In 2011, David Lynch was recruited to capture the essence of Dom Pérignon Rosé Vintage 2000.

Among all these testimonials, Marlene Dietrich's perhaps stands out as the most elegant. "Champagne has an extraordinary symbolic impact," she used to say. "You suddenly feel like it's Sunday, and that better times are just ahead. If you manage to get a properly cooled bottle of Dom Pérignon served in a pretty glass on the terrace of a Paris restaurant with a view of the trees on a sunny day in early fall, you'll feel like the most divine being in the world, even if you're accustomed to drinking champagne." It would be hard to put it better. Marilyn Monroe was another fan of Dom Pérignon in her own way, expressed with heartfelt spontaneity, unceremoniously. For Monroe, it represented a fleeting moment of happiness and pleasure to be seized from the chaotic flow of life, whether on the set, during a photo shoot, or in the middle of costume fittings (such as the ones required by Hollywood fashion designer Jean-Louis to complete, over many weeks, the unforgettable stole of silk, beads, and sequins (at a cost of $12,000) that she wore to President John F. Kennedy's birthday party at Madison Square Garden in 1962, an appearance witnessed by a dazzled American public.

It was in 1959, during another party in New York, that Marilyn burst through the throng with a glass of champagne, and handed it to a young Danish scriptwriter, Hans Jørgen Lembourn, whom she had met a few days earlier. "Here," she said,

"I'll get another one for myself. It's Dom Pérignon, my favorite champagne." Lembourn recounted this meeting—and the whirlwind affair that followed—in his *Diary of a Lover of Marilyn Monroe*. It was brief, impulsive, almost childish affair, forty days in quest of love, one of the most precious moments being an escape to the hills in a car with a stock of Dom Pérignon, which served as a lucky charm or magic potion. At first Marilyn remained curled in the corner of the front seat, not saying a word. Then she leaned over and began rummaging

Richard Geoffroy, cellar master and creator of Dom Pérignon's vintage wines since 1996, turns to his distant predecessor for inspiration.

through all the stuff scattered on the back seat. She pulled out a bottle of Dom Pérignon, opened the glove compartment, and took out two plastic glasses. She removed the wire and cap, popped the cork and tossed it out the car as the froth flew away in the wind. She filled the glasses, handed one to Lembourn, and downed her own in two or three long swallows, then filled it again and stuck the bottle between her knees. She held her glass in one hand, and with the other she clutched the brim of her extravagant hat. "Now we're on vacation," she said.

In order to continue filling this "visitor's book" with new entries, Richard Geoffroy, who has been cellar master and creator of Dom Pérignon's vintage wines since 1996, turns to his distant predecessor, Dom Pierre Pérignon ("the father of champagne") for inspiration. It is a spirit that Geoffroy regularly rediscovers in the wonderful setting of the abbey itself. "The abbey's heritage is spiritual as well as technical," he says. "Inspiration

FACING PAGE: *The sparkling wine made in Champagne was already famous in the seventeeth century, as witnessed by this detail from* The Wine Drinkers *a painting by Jacques Autreau (1657–1745), now in the Louvre (top). A portrait of young King Louis XIV, aged sixteen or so, by Charles Lebrun (bottom, left); the king's table at Versailles served "the best wine in the world," namely the one made by Dom Pérignon. In the château of Versailles, the luminous Salon of Peace can be glimpsed from the Hall of Mirrors (bottom, right).*

comes to me when I walk the grounds and connect with this place in the sole goal of remaining faithful to the traces of the original Dom Pérignon." In order to perform his main task—the constantly renewed challenge of making vintage wine— Geoffroy obeys rules that are almost as constraining as those of Saint Benedict. His monk-like fidelity has resulted in ten rules that Geoffroy calls his "Manifesto." It represents an artistic vision, setting out the creative path to follow in order to produce a work of art: Dom Pérignon, white or pink, can only be made into vintage wine if there is a clear determination to recount a new story each year (obviously in a consistent style and spirit), even if that means renouncing a vintage wine in certain years; the wine must be an assemblage, because assemblage is a key factor in establishing a style, yet there can be only one assemblage of white and one assemblage of rosé per year, because there can only be one ideal interpretation of a given year; the assemblage must aim for a perfect balance between Chardonnay and Pinot Noir grapes, one that generates resonance and tension; Dom Pérignon can only be made with the finest products of Champagne, namely nine essential, top-ranked growths (including the legendary Hautvillers *premier cru*), sometimes rising to seventeen grand growths; respect for the soil and climate must be total, and the wine must be made without artifice, the goal being to exalt the original freshness of the fruit even in the assemblage process; the intensity of Dom Pérignon stems neither from strength or force but from a precise, "high-definition" quality that rings true rather than hitting hard; Dom Pérignon's salient characteristic is its "touch," the way it feels in the mouth—a ripe, airy freshness, a silky or even creamy texture, and a thoroughly integrated effervescence; the incomparable complexity and ageing potential of wine requires long maturation on lees, remaining at least seven years in the cellar; Dom Pérignon's mineral quality represents its deliberate aromatic signature, at once earthy, ocean-salty, grilled, smoky and peaty; the uniqueness of the Dom Pérignon style makes it a mysterious, paradoxical champagne, simultaneously rhythmic and precise, fresh and complex.

In the year 2000, Dom Pérignon began a new chapter in its history when Richard Geoffroy launched a collection of old vintage champagnes dubbed "Oenothèque." After many months of tasting old vintage champagnes stored in the firm's cellars, Geoffroy noted that certain thresholds of aging reliably yielded surprising and delicious new developments in the wine: after twelve to fifteen years, sometimes extending up to twenty, the champagne reaches a second level of fullness and delivers its original qualities with even greater intensity, along with added depth and elaborate notes of malt and chocolate. Then, beyond twenty years, the champagne acquires a new dimension, a third level of fullness, when it changes register, having distilled its aromas into scents of sandalwood, musk, tobacco, and truffles. Its texture meanwhile is concentrated and penetrating yet airy. The selection of these ancient wonders is a task that Geoffroy has found as exciting as the two other high points of his job, namely, the blending and tasting operations that determine whether or not a given year will be declared "vintage."

FACING PAGE: *In the eighteenth century, during the reign of Louis XV,* le vin de Champagne *was highly fashionable not only in France but also at the courts of England, Germany, and Russia.* The Prince de Conti's Supper in the Temple Palace, *painted by Michel Barthélemy Ollivier in 1766, features "coolers" in the foreground where the wine was held.*

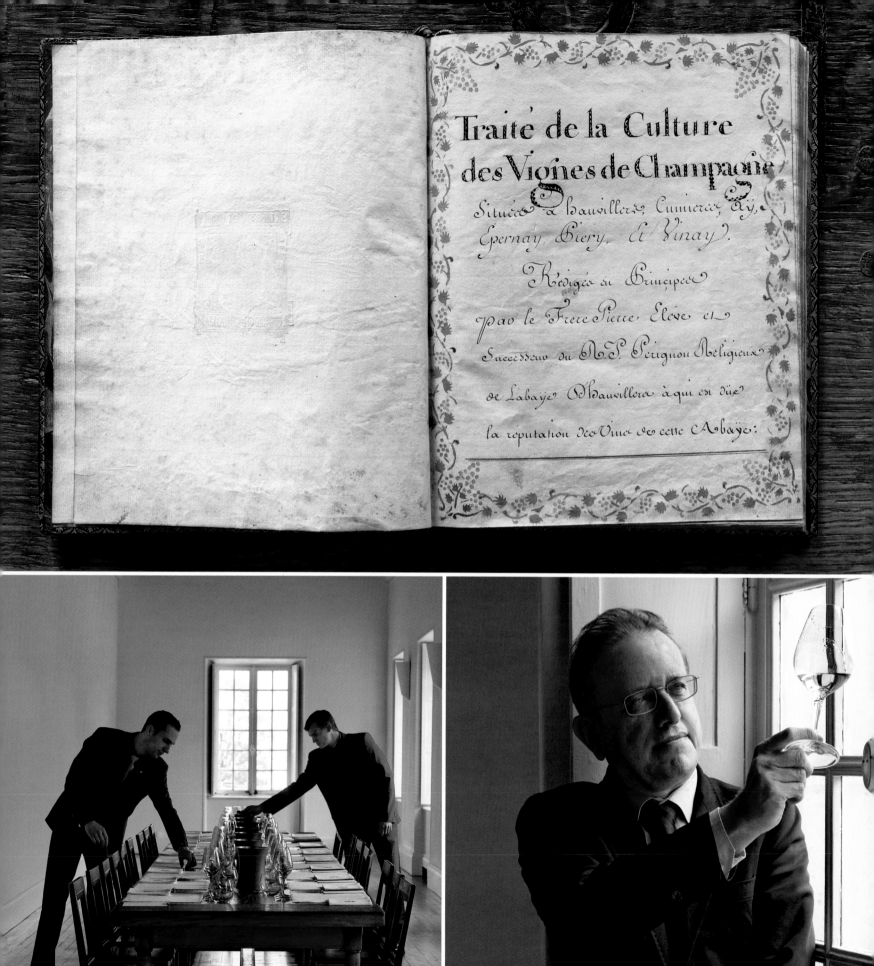

Traité de la Culture
des Vignes de Champagne
Située à Hauvillers, Cumieres, Ay,
Epernay, Piery, & Vinay.

Rédigée en Principes

par le Frere Pierre Elève et

Successeur du R.P. Perignon Religieux

de Labaye d'Hauvillers à qui en due

la reputation des Vins de cette Abaye:

AROUND THE WORLD IN SEARCH OF NEW HARMONIES

Geoffroy does not go to the abbey of Hautvillers solely to meditate. He regularly holds tastings there, inviting professionals to share meals where harmonious new marriages between champagne and various dishes can be assessed. He brokers these marriages with some of the greatest chefs in the world; the likes of Guy Savoy, Alain Ducasse, Alain Senderens, Joël Rebuchon, Heston Blumenthal, Jean-François Piège, and Hervé This. Geoffroy doesn't choose these chefs because they're famous, but because they are passionate about his wines and because contact with their great culinary creativity constantly leads beyond standard frontiers and conventional expectations.

Contacts, encounters, voyages: one of the most fascinating characteristics of Dom Pérignon seems to arise from a dialectic, or even clash, between two worlds, two sensibilities. From these, new and surprising harmonies of food and wine are born. There is no more striking example of this approach than the truly creative accomplishments of Dom Pérignon's own house chef, Pascal Tingaud, who managed to exorcise some traditional taboos with respect to champagne, namely artichokes, asparagus, and chocolate. Long reflection and meticulous preparation enabled Tingaud to transform a potential conflict of flavors into new taste sensations.

In his poem "The Voyage," Baudelaire urged us to "fathom the unknown to find the *new!*" It is a good illustration of the fruitful encounters triggered by travel, by discovery of the world's cuisines and their ability to exalt wine. Now Dom Pérignon champagne is voyaging as never before, even without leaving Épernay or Hautvillers. A few privileged guests—sommeliers and culinary journalists from the world over,

assembled for one of the regular "Dom Pérignon seminars"—will never forget, for instance, the magical union between a Dom Pérignon 1973 with a pigeon *à l'accouchée*, a kind of Moroccan pigeon stew. In this dish, the pigeon is stuffed with a mixture of garlic, onion, and *smen*, the clarified butter used in oriental cuisine, which is aged in an earthenware pot. The pigeon is then slowly braised for several hours in poultry stock flavored with a blend of five Moroccan spices, known as *ras el hanout*. "What? Garlic with champagne?" Dinner guests were initially alarmed at the combination. Garlic with champagne indeed, but garlic that has been well cooked to make it mild and creamy, leaving it open to the sensuous caress of the lightly toasted flavors of a great champagne with its hints of ripe plum and subtle citrus.

Even more surprising, yet another voyage led Dom Pérignon to the age-old Japanese tradition of *kaiseki*, which likens the preparation and tasting of a meal to the spiritual experience of communing with nature. Geoffroy invited the great chef Yoshio Murata from the renowned Kyoto restaurant Kikunoi to a *kaiseki* dinner with Dom Pérignon. Not since the days when the music of bubbles mingled with the prayers of monks has champagne met such fervent palates. On the menu that day: roe wrapped in sea bream and sprinkled with seaweed vinegar, steamed rice and caviar, and grilled abalone in abalone-liver sauce.

In 2011, over the course of several trips to Hong Kong during which he gathered five chefs from different regions of China, Richard Geoffroy refined what he intended as Dom Pérignon's tribute to Chinese culture—a banquet that features the country's main culinary traditions (Cantonese, Pekinese, Szechuan, Yunnan, etc.) accompanied by some well-chosen vintages for a festive, friendly evening. For the first time, highly demanding culinary criteria brought China and Dom Pérignon together. Planned for thirty guests, the meal

FACING PAGE: *The first page of a "Treatise on Growing Vines in Champagne" copied by Friar Pierre, Dom Pierre Pérignon's successor (top). This remarkable eighteenth-century manuscript, written on vellum, could be considered the earliest technical manual on working the vineyards in Champagne. In the spare setting of the cloister's former library, a table is set for a tasting of old champagnes (bottom, left). Tastings are done under the aegis of cellar master Richard Geoffroy, who draws his inspiration and impeccable standards from these timeless premises, where the spirit of Dom Pérignon himself is still present (bottom, right).*

respected the traditional order of a Chinese banquet. The warmth, fruitiness, and depth of a Dom Pérignon Vintage 2002 accompanied not only the hors d'oeuvre (which included scallops with ginger and spring onions cooked on the shell, sweet shrimp with tea leaves and vinegar, a sea-urchin flan, pigeon eggs with rice wine from Shaoxing, and clam sashimi), but also the fish-bladder soup. The second bottle, an already legendary Dom Pérignon Oenothèque Vintage 1996, was uncorked for the next course of the banquet: lobster in black bean sauce, whole grouper cooked in steam, and tofu with asparagus and shrimp eggs. The final dishes were accompanied by the mildly spicy and smoky notes, with overtones of grapefruit, of a Dom Pérignon Rosé 2000: dried abalone and sea cucumbers in black sauce, crunchy pigeon marinated in fermented taro root, consommé of pigeon and foie gras, and pigeon eggs with smoky tea. Dessert, also enjoyed with the pink Dom Pérignon, was steamed double bird's nest with osmanthus flower and lotus seeds. Finally, the startling Yunnan tea known as Pu Erh—the only tea that is aged, hence sometimes sold according to vintage years— had a finesse and mildness that brought to mind the aromatic palette of a few Dom Pérignon Oenothèque vintages much older than the tea itself.

Two years earlier, the same magnificent, sophisticated setting of a traditional banquet characterized another voyage—a trip back in time. After long historical research, Michelin-starred chef Jean-François Piège conceived a series of dinners. In order to relive the days when Louis XIV in Versailles first tasted the "best wine in the world" (made by the king's exact contemporary, Dom Pierre Pérignon), the "Sun King's Table" was faithfully recreated on the site of Versailles itself. After tidbits served in a salon of Versailles château accompanied by Dom Pérignon Vintage 1995, the guests—thirty food journalists from all over the world—were invited into the Antechamber of the

A few privileged guests—sommeliers and culinary journalists from the world over, assembled for one of the regular "Dom Pérignon seminars"— will never forget, for instance, the magical marriage of a Dom Pérignon 1973 with a pigeon à l'accouchée, *a kind of Moroccan pigeon stew.*

Grand Dinner Service, where the king ate his meals. The table was laid according to authentic details of the day, including damask tablecloth and "barleycorn" glasses recreated for the occasion by the Bayel crystal firm.

The meal was scrupulously faithful to French royal traditions of the seventeenth century. This fantastic time machine was accompanied throughout by one of Dom Pérignon's sunniest vintages, an Oenothèque 1976. That year's heatwave resulted in exceptionally ripe grapes as early as September 1. The champagne's warm, powerful bouquet features notes of honeysuckle followed by ripe plums and raisins, evolving into complex aromas with toasty overtones. In the mouth, the rich nectar maintains a balance between mildness and strength, between plenitude and depth. Its length in the mouth seems to challenge the clock—as did the meal itself—a challenge brought to a brilliant close by a final, sweetly bitter hint of blood oranges. This warm, luminous champagne was served in the traditional Versailles manner—not poured at the table but brought in a glass to each guest by a waiter. And it was chosen for its ability to enlighten highly varied sensations, triggered by the four traditional "courses" of a royal dinner featuring dishes of that period.

PAGES 78–79: *An inside page of the manuscript showing the village of Cumières and the woods and vineyards around the abbey of Hautvillers, seen in the foreground right of the picture.*
FACING PAGE: *In the timeless atmosphere of the cellars, vintage wines age for no less than seven years (ten, fifteen, and sometimes twenty or more) as their aromas and flavors mature. Their powerful ageing potential enabled Richard Geoffroy to launch the Dom Pérignon Vintage Collection in 2000.*
PAGE 83: *Time weaves its protective web in the sanctity of the wine cellar.*

At Dom Pérignon we are completely committed
to vintage champagne—the entire output is vintage.
That's not a market strategy, but a commitment:
vintage champagne calls for a very special philosophy,
which is in Dom Pérignon's genes. The real challenge
for us is to transform the constraints of any given year into an
opportunity. We must find a point of encounter between the specific
character of a year and Dom Pérignon's own uniqueness, which carries
a certain risk. Dom Pérignon always walks a tightrope—a vintage will
only succeed if it has some extra soul, transcendence. It's an act of
creation. Therein lies the rarity of Dom Pérignon. Every vintage
champagne is original while always remaining Dom Pérignon.
Which is why Dom Pérignon cannot be made every single year.
Dom Pérignon draws from vintage wine the strength to reinvent
itself, the opportunity to challenge and transcend itself.

———————

Richard Geoffroy
CELLAR MASTER

Tasting notes

VINTAGE: Dom Pérignon 2003
HARVEST: A long hot summer called for one of the earliest harvests ever; perfectly ripe
and healthy grapes reached an ideal stage of maturity.
FIRST NOSE: Sweet floral notes evolve toward a mineral quality; notes of candied fruit,
the freshness of camphor leaves; finally, hints of spices and licorice.
ATTACK IN MOUTH: Vibrant. A sweet smoothness extends into a final note that is slightly bitter
and saline with a blush of iodine.
PERFECT COMBINATIONS: Sea urchins, scallops, smoked eel, abalone; also white truffle.

The first course consisted of "hors-d'oeuvre" (game, paté in crust, seafood and shellfish) followed by soups (beef, chestnut and truffle, shellfish and mushroom, and pumpkin). The second course was composed of roasts (scallops, wild duck, hare, beef and smoked eel, wild salmon). The third course featured side dishes (salads, rice, mushroom soufflé, iced cheese, hard-boiled eggs). The fourth course was dessert in the form of a witty, edible "candle" of chocolate. This magnificent dinner with its savor of history was followed by an after-dinner treat of Dom Pérignon Vintage 2000 accompanied by sweet tidbits (such as tiny madeleines that made for a literarily memorable evening).

The wonderful quality of such wines naturally leads to noble foods, ones that symbolize a grand tradition, region, or culture. Take, for example, the most precious of all truffles, the white truffle from Alba, so venerated in the Piedmont for its concentrated, earthy power and its unique flavor; when discussing it, some people detect hints of cabbage, fennel, walnuts, even leather and earth. Yet what's the point of such comparisons? In the end, a white truffle delivers nothing other than the flavor and aromas of white truffle, which are incomparably simple and delicious. But Geoffroy likes the white truffle precisely because it speaks only of itself, of its own purity and simplicity. These are exactly the qualities that Dom Pérignon champagne can ennoble and enrich.

This highly original quest for perfect harmony can be expanded to include other rare foods such as various caviars or cured Spanish hams like *pata negra puro bellota* (made from black pigs fed on green acorns). But the crowning discovery of such research perhaps came from a pure, venerable product that, like wine, is a symbol of European civilization, which no one had yet dared to marry with champagne: olive oil. After countless tastings,

The meal was scrupulously faithful to French royal traditions of the seventeenth century. This fantastic time machine was accompanied throughout by one of Dom Pérignon's sunniest vintages, an Oenothèque 1976.

it transpired that only one olive oil—an ardent, green oil from Sicily—could trigger a glorious encounter with Dom Pérignon. Images of these rare harmonies, and miraculous marriages, will fill the head of visitors strolling through the grounds of the abbey of Hautvillers in the heart of the Champagne district, conjuring up a secret Mediterranean. The vast terrace overlooking the Marne, draped in vines, could well be in Tuscany, the imposing gray cedars could stand on Mount Lebanon, while the bucolic shepherd's hut below a row of linden trees has a Virgilian air.

In 2007, the appearance of Dom Pérignon Vintage 1999 inspired chef Tingaud to attempt another, ambitious kind of voyage, a new way to demonstrate all the riches of a wine. Thanks to seven meticulously chosen and prepared dishes, the seven striking facets of Vintage 1999—profound yet airy, mature yet luminous in a way that the cellar master rightly called "theatrical and dramatic"—would be revealed in turn. A unique tasting session was organized in seven stages. First came the Vintage 1999's "profound" character, brought out by Aquitaine caviar eaten either straight or prepared with an avocado cream; then three dishes subtly underscored the note of "iodine" in the wine, namely clam *dashi* (Japanese broth), oyster with a dash of fresh ginger, and a risotto with cuttlefish ink. A Thai soup

FACING PAGE: *A view from the Hall of Mirrors in Versailles, overlooking the grand canal (top). In 2009 Michelin-starred chef Jean-François Piège recreated the "Sun King's Table" by serving highly select guests the four traditional "courses" of a royal meal in the Antechamber of the Grand Dinner Service. In consultation with the cellar master, house chef Pascal Tingaud employs his talent to innovate by breaking culinary taboos (bottom, left). He works with new ingredients and flavors drawn from Spanish, Mexican, Thai, Chinese, and Japanese gastronomy. The ultimate goal is to reveal the infinite aromatic intensity and profoundly universal nature of Dom Pérignon. Wakame seaweed is a favorite ingredient of Japanese cuisine (bottom, right).*

Chef Pascal Tingaud's Recipe

Sea Bass Steamed over Seaweed

INGREDIENTS
Serves 4

- 1 sea bass weighing 3 ¼ lb. (1.5 kg)
- 1 teaspoon fine salt
- 2 small pieces ginger root, grated
- 1 bunch cilantro, leaves picked
- 2 tablespoons soy sauce
- 1 tablespoon Shao Xing (Chinese rice wine) or white vermouth
- 2 onions, finely sliced
- 3 ½ oz. (100 g) wakame seaweed
- A good pinch of kosher salt
- 12 drops sesame oil

METHOD

Gut the fish, leaving the head and tail. Scrape off the scales and wash under cold water. Pat dry carefully with paper towel.

Make fairly deep diagonal incisions about ¾ inch (1.5 cm) apart on each side of the fish. Rub it inside and outside with the salt. In each incision, place some grated ginger and cilantro leaves, leaving some for decoration. Drizzle the soy sauce and Shao Xing over the fish.

Arrange the sliced onions in the steamer basket and carefully place the fish over the onions.

Place the water in the steam cooker and add the seaweed and salt. Bring to the boil. Steam the fish for 10 to 15 minutes. The flesh must remain firm to the touch.

Heat the sesame oil. When it is smoking, drizzle it over the fish and sprinkle it with the reserved cilantro leaves.

Serve very hot.

of crayfish with citronella leaf and coconut then awakened a "powdery-nacreous" impression in the palate, while the "brilliance" of the champagne emerged wonderfully from a straightforward encounter with a fruit, grenadilla, here sparked with a dot of Espelette pepper; the fully "tactile" quality of the Vintage 1999 was then appreciated with an extraordinary Italian ham known as *culatello*, aged for up to twenty-six months in the northern part of Parma. Then the wine's obvious "intensity" resonated thanks to crayfish with a touch of black mole (a traditional Mexican sauce from Oaxaca requiring some forty ingredients, with vegetal, peppery notes of aniseed). The seventh and last facet, the wine's "complexity," involved black mole once again, but this time in a major key, poured over a rare, tender piece of pigeon that focused all the wine's vegetal, fruity, peppery freshness.

This unique event, designed to reveal all the facets of one particular champagne, was repeated the following year with Dom Pérignon Vintage 2000. Even more than other vintage champagnes, the Vintage 2000 expresses Dom Pérignon's double nature—its rigor and generosity, its clarity and its profuseness. This time the seven moments of grace were accompanied by Pu Erh (an aged tea), by fruit and vegetables (iced ficoid, Japanese white radish, rambutan, green mango), scallop carpaccio, cod with peach and truffle sauce, grilled eggplant with honey and spices, pigeon *à l'accouchée*, a combination of caviar, barley with argan oil and saffron ice cream, and finally a little Thai-rice pudding with coconut ash. Fifteen French and foreign chefs from around the world attended this tasting, in order to assimilate the basic principles and apply them at their own restaurants. On this occasion, Dom Pérignon proved that it was not only the rarest of champagnes, but also, thanks to its infinite richness, intensity, and above all harmony, the most profoundly universal.

The warmth, fruitiness, and depth of a Dom Pérignon Vintage 2002 accompanied not only the hors d'oeuvre, but also scallops with ginger and spring onions cooked on the shell.

PAGE 86: *Sea bass steamed over wakame seaweed, a recipe created by Dom Pérignon chef Pascal Tingaud. This blend of French and Japanese culinary traditions features the generous mineral aromas that characterize Dom Pérignon Vintage 2002 (facing page).*

Champagne

VEUVE CLICQUOT

Champagne

V euve Clicquot is the only champagne associated with one specific color—a striking yellow. The color was initially used in the latter half of the nineteenth century on a new label to identify a particular style then designated by the English term "dry"; today it is found on almost all Veuve Clicquot bottles. This deep yellow hue conveys vitality, dynamism, and energy. In fact, its harmonious blend of strength and delicacy is characteristic not only of Veuve Clicquot champagne, but above all of the widow Clicquot herself.

Madame Clicquot was born Barbe Nicole Ponsardin on December 16, 1777. Her father, Nicolas, was a well-known textile manufacturer in Reims, and a powerful figure in the city. Elevated to the rank of baron during Napoleon's empire, he was mayor of Reims from 1810 until his death in 1820, and chairman of the local chamber of commerce. Barbe Nicole married François Clicquot in 1798; then aged twenty-four, the young man had studied business in Switzerland and had just joined his father, Philippe Clicquot, in the family concern. Like many pioneers in the champagne industry, Philippe was a cloth merchant who also became a banker, landowner, and, from 1792 onward, a wine merchant. When young François became his

father's partner shortly after his marriage, Clicquot champagne was already being enjoyed in Italy, Germany, Switzerland, Belgium, and Russia. In addition to its quality, the wine could be identified by the mark of a ship's anchor branded on the base of the cork, a logo that the firm has never abandoned. François expanded the business even further, specializing in champagne and traveling extensively. In 1801, in Basel, Switzerland, he hired a traveling agent named Louis Bohne, who would later become a close adviser to Madame Clicquot. One year later, Philippe Clicquot retired and left the running of the firm, renamed "Clicquot et Fils," to François. In subsequent years Bohne traveled all across Europe as far as Russia, which would soon become the company's main foreign outlet.

François Clicquot died young, in 1805. His widow decided to run the business. In the early nineteenth century it required a great deal of courage and audacity for a young woman of twenty-seven, mother of a young daughter, Clémentine, to become head of an enterprise that operated in an already highly competitive market. Since a woman could only head a company on an interim basis—between two generations of males— the firm changed its name to Veuve ("Widow")

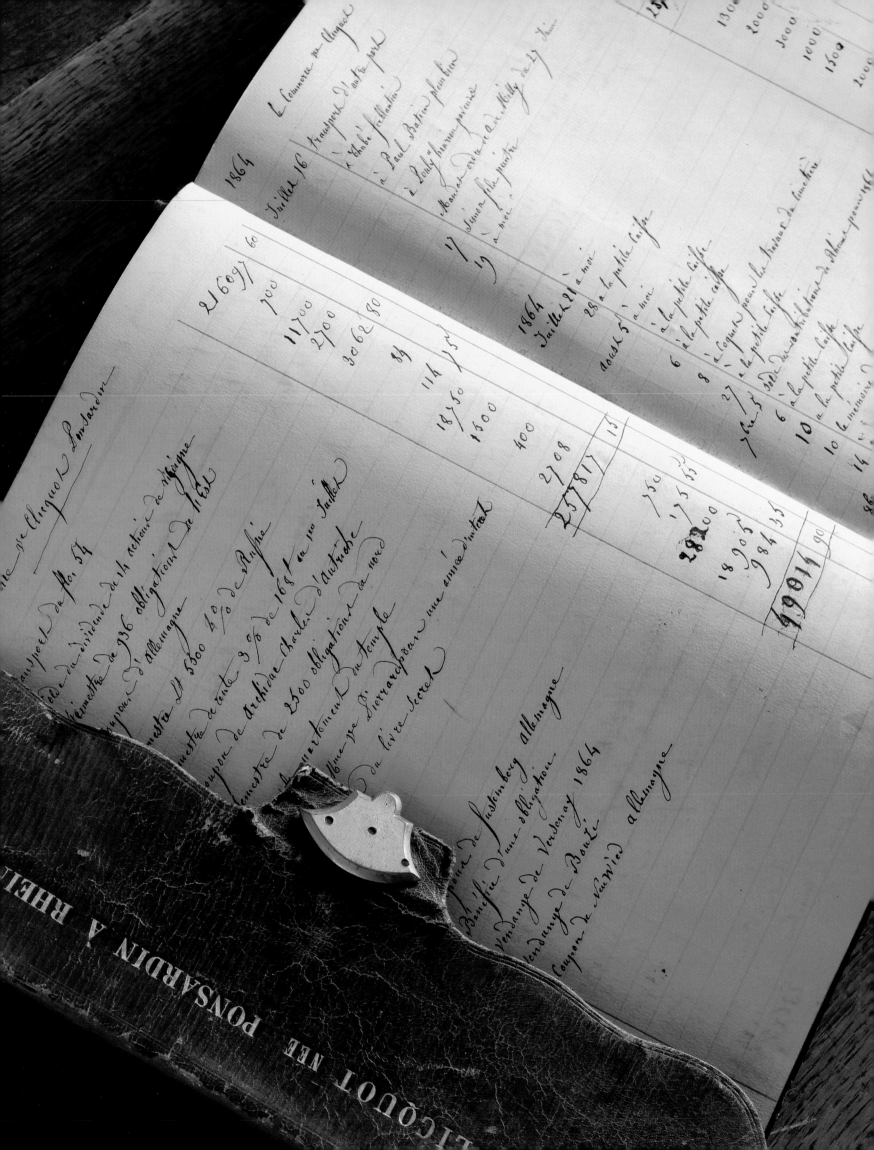

Clicquot Ponsardin, making it today the oldest brand to bear a woman's name.

Madame Clicquot was a fast learner. Recent archive evidence proves that as early as 1810, after tastings and assemblages, she produced a vintage champagne, one of the earliest attested vintages in the Champagne region. Another stroke of genius dates from 1814. Napoleon had just abdicated, and on April 6 the imperial senate summoned Louis XVIII to the French throne. No traders thought of re-establishing contact with Russia, the erstwhile enemy, so soon—except Madame Clicquot. She wanted to get there first, and was ready in a matter of weeks. Thus on June 6 the ship *Gebroders* sailed from Le Havre for Königsberg and Saint Petersburg carrying ten thousand, five hundred bottles of Veuve Clicquot champagne, which included the legendary vintage of 1811 dubbed the "Comet Wine." Having been deprived of champagne for several years, the Russians snapped up the Veuve Clicquot, found it delightful, and remained faithful to it. The Russian market never looked back. Less than half a century later, when the likes of Pushkin, Chekhov, and Gogol were lauding Veuve Clicquot champagnes, the French novelist, Prosper Mérimée, wrote: "Madame Clicquot quenches Russia's thirst. Her wine is called Klikofskoé, and no other champagne is drunk there."

Russia made the widow Clicquot's fortune in no time. By 1819, she was delivering over one hundred thousand bottles annually to the country. To her shrewd business sense Madame Clicquot soon added a keen awareness of the importance of the quality of her wines. "One quality alone, the best!" was her motto. She took an interest in the way champagne was made, notably the process of clarifying the wine, which she revolutionized in 1816 by developing the riddling board, an inspired invention later imitated by all champagne makers. Nearly a century later, in 2005, Andrée Putman, the "grand lady of design," was inspired by Madame Clicquot's ingenuity to transform the rustic riddling board into a contemporary yet romantic table that evokes the various stages of the process devised two centuries earlier. The table is accompanied by two chairs, perfect for a private little wine tasting.

Ever since 1972 the Veuve Clicquot Award has been presented to the most remarkable women in the world. The prize is open to women from any sphere whose boldness and creativity are reminiscent of Madame Clicquot. The winner is allocated a special vine in the Verzy vineyard, which henceforth bears her name.

In 1821 Madame Clicquot hired a new employee, Édouard Werlé. A German orphan then aged twenty, Werlé soon perfected his French and familiarized himself with the business, becoming managing director in 1826 and a partner five years later. He expanded business considerably, doubling the volume of sales in a decade. In 1840, on a plot he bought from Madame Clicquot near the cathedral in the center of Reims, Werlé built an elegant private residence, the hôtel du Marc. Neo-classical in style, the building still serves as the company's most glamorous reception venue.

What did Veuve Clicquot Ponsardin champagne actually taste like in the second quarter of the nineteenth century, when business was booming and Madame Clicquot was at the height of her art? Thanks to an amazing discovery, we now know

PAGE 94: *Bound in Morocco leather, the last personal account ledger written in the hand of the Widow Clicquot (née Ponsardin).*
PAGE 95: *On the upper floor of the hôtel du Marc is a portrait of Madame Clicquot and her great granddaughter Anne, the future duchess of Uzès. It was painted around 1860–62 by the widow's official artist, Léon Cogniet. On the right of the painting is a sketch of magnificent château of Borsault—inspired by the royal château of Chambord—that Madame Clicquot built in 1843 to the west of Épernay on heights overlooking the Marne River. That is where she died in July 1866.*
FACING PAGE: *A view of the large greenhouse on the Verzy estate (top). This is where grafts of young vine plants were traditionally carried out up to the 1970s. The title page of an 1857 vineyard survey of grand-cru plots in Bouzy that belonged to Veuve Clicquot (bottom, right).*

the answer. On July 16, 2010, divers discovered a shipwreck at the bottom of the Baltic Sea, 175 feet deep. There they found forty-seven bottles of Veuve Clicquot champagne, the oldest known bottles in existence. The wine has entranced those lucky enough to taste it. Only slightly effervescent, it is amply dosed with sugar, as was the custom at the time. Over a century and a half old, this champagne now has "a nose of toasty, spicy aromas with a hint of coffee, and has a thoroughly pleasant taste with floral notes and overtones of citrus fruit." The unplanned storage conditions turned out to be ideal: a pressure of six bars, a constant temperature of 5°C (44°F), and total darkness. Most of the bottles are in excellent condition and the natural aging process has considerably slowed. So we are now familiar with the wine Madame Clicquot made toward the end of her career.

The widow Clicquot died in her château de Boursault on July 29, 1866. Her heirs received the company assets, the buildings, and the vineyards. The name of Veuve Clicquot, however, already belonged to Werlé in accordance with an agreement made by the two partners some time earlier.

He continued to build the business enthusiastically, modernizing production techniques and transportation, extending international trade, and devising the famous yellow label in 1877. Werlé's descendents owned and ran Veuve Clicquot Ponsardin until the firm was bought in 1986 by Louis Vuitton (which became LVMH in 1987). Today the champagne company is run by Jean-Marc Lacave.

Another residence owned by Veuve Clicquot is Verzy manor, built in the early nineteenth century. With its waxed parquet floors, old-fashioned tiling, fabrics, country furniture, and curtains in warm colors (largely orange-yellow), the manor is located in the heart of Montagne de Reims and has a magnificent view of the endless vineyards. Nearby, a large plot planted with Chardonnay grapes has

With its waxed parquet floors, old-fashioned tiling, fabrics, country furniture, and curtains in warm colors, Verzy manor is located in the heart of Montagne de Reims and has a magnificent view of the endless vineyards.

been assigned a special role, and is dedicated to influential women: ever since 1972 the Veuve Clicquot Award has been presented to the most remarkable women in the world. The prize is open to women in thirty countries across the globe and it rewards socially conscious growth, going to a woman from any sphere whose boldness and creativity are reminiscent of Madame Clicquot. The winner is allocated a special vine in the Verzy vineyard, which henceforth bears her name.

Veuve Clicquot is a delightfully paradoxical establishment. Passionately faithful to its extraordinary history, as recorded not only in its archives but also in its fine residences and wonderful chalk-quarry cellars, it is also the most dynamic and most audacious of businesses, always in step with the times. "Clicquot yellow" is the color of forthright modernity, expressed through the design of handsome accessories that always reflect boldness, and often humor. The Veuve Clicquot image sparkles in wonderfully offbeat items such as bottle jackets and ice buckets.
The firm also calls upon leading designers who translate its elegance and boldness into often spectacular projects: Karim Rashid designed a Loveseat, while the Porsche Design Studio created Vertical Limit, an extraordinary champagne rack

PAGES 98–99: *The Verzy manor, covered in Virginia creeper, was bought in 1902. Throughout the year it hosts company guests from all over the world, including wine experts, specialized journalists, wine stewards, famous chefs, and enlightened connoisseurs. The entrance gate is decorated with the firm's first logo, an anchor with the widow's initials, VCP. Originally, in the seventeenth century, this mark was branded on the bottom of the corks, enabling Madame Clicquot to authenticate her own champagne. It remains a company emblem to this day.*
FACING PAGE: *A view of the entrance hall of Verzy manor, a nineteenth-century residence with rustic charm.*

I find it really exciting to recreate the Clicquot
style every year, to maintain the reliable house style through
the blending of a range of wines that are very different from year
to year. Making vintage champagnes is more creative—it's a
question of seduction. You have let yourself be seduced by what
the year has to offer. At Veuve Clicquot, the proportions between
Pinot Noir, Pinot Meunier, and Chardonnay slightly differ from
the Brut version. The Pinot must express itself fully. The palette
can vary so much from year to year! When creating a vintage
champagne, the cellar master takes greater risks. Veuve Clicquot's
2002 and 2004 vintages are very different. Customers might
wonder about that, but wine stewards greatly appreciate vintage
champagnes in terms of potential culinary combinations.
Vintage wines are important from a gastronomic standpoint.
They make it possible to transcend expectations.

———

Dominique Demarville
CELLAR MASTER

Tasting notes

VINTAGE: Vintage 2004
HARVEST: An outstanding September!
ASSEMBLAGE: 62 percent Pinot Noir — 30 percent Chardonnay — 8 percent Pinot Meunier.
DOSAGE: 7 grams per liter
FIRST NOSE: Aromas of crunchy fresh fruit and citrus fruit, followed by a mineral note. Scents of
violet and lilac merge with "confectionary" aromas (hazelnut, quince jelly).
ATTACK IN MOUTH: Straightforward, generous, and dynamic.
PERFECT COMBINATIONS: Fresh-water fish, shellfish (crayfish, lobster), and white meat.

in the form of a futurist steel monolith, produced in a limited edition of fifteen. Tom Dixon, meanwhile, drew inspiration from both the DesignBox (Veuve Clicquot's environmentally friendly paper case) and the historic Comet emblem when designing his highly romantic Comet Lamp. Then there are the Campana brothers, who produced the spectacular Gloriette in the grounds of the hôtel Marc in Reims.

This modernity, in conjunction with great elegance and traditional heritage, has been evident in the hôtel du Marc since 2011, after four years of patient restoration. The idea was not only to restore its original luster while adding modern touches that would make distinguished guests more comfortable, but also to significantly lighten its carbon footprint. A bold choice of renewable energies (geothermal and solar), low-energy lighting, and the thermal use of unused cellars has resulted in a sixty-five percent reduction in energy consumption and a ninety percent drop in the emission of greenhouse gases. The renovation project was awarded to Bruno Moinard for his highly personal and clearly refined method of interpreting the history of these premises.

Like all family homes, the hôtel du Marc seeks to encourage creativity among its friends and relations. Everyone in Veuve Clicquot's select circle has wanted to leave a mark or souvenir, so today the residence is dotted with original creations by artists and designers. Once past the threshold with its translucent, dark-glass festooned canopy, the entrance hall features a château-style floor of white paving studded with black cabochons. The residence's role of host is underscored by its two-tiered layout: one path leads upstairs via a grand staircase while another leads to the reception salons. Beneath the staircase a screen made of fine strips of mirror, seemingly pleated like a piece of Fortuny silk, reflects a fragmented landscape—it has been dubbed "the kaleidoscope" for its highly poetic interplay of light and color.

Visitors who are staying the night are led up the grand staircase. Right from the first step the hôtel du Marc is an ode to vineyards, to the seasons, and to the colors of champagne. Opposite the original banister another banister is attached to the sand-colored wall. Wiry like a vine stock,

Veuve Clicquot is the only champagne associated with one specific color—a striking yellow. The color was initially used in the latter half of the nineteenth century on a new label to identify a particular style then designated by the English term "dry."

it emerges from the wall then plunges back into the stone only to emerge again a few inches further along. This artwork by Pablo Reinoso completes its mad race on the upper floor, sinking like a root into a window box that extends into a seat. Indeed, nothing is so pleasant as musing on a bench or reading beneath a tree, waiting for friends to return from a jaunt in the vineyards. But a long hallway urges guests to reach their bedrooms, its theatrical lighting shed not by traditional lamps but by paintings. Padding quietly down this gallery of portraits on golden coconut matting, visitors parade before the eyes of Louis Bohne, the duchess of Uzès, and others.

The bedrooms in the hôtel du Marc are an ode to the seasonal cycle of vineyards and winemaking. Some of them have a view of another company property, the Muire Pavilion. Built in 1656 for the nobleman Nicolas Noël de Muire , this Italianate pavilion is one of the few surviving Renaissance buildings in Reims. Other bedrooms overlook the

50
Lettres
Françaises

du 3 Juillet 1880
au 8 Septembre —if

51
Lettres
Françaises

du 9 Septembre 1880
au 3 Novembre —if

52
Lettres
Françaises

du 4 Novembre 1880
au 28 Décembre —if

53
Lettres
Françaises

du 28 Décembre 1880
au 11 Février 1881

grounds with its weeping beech and maple trees. The decor of each room was devised according to the life and tastes of the illustrious character who inspired it. To take just two examples, the "Louis Bohne" bedroom is predominantly blue with a block of crystal that serves as a bench at the foot of the bed, evoking the Russian winters—with rivers often choked with ice—that Bohne, the intrepid traveler, often had to face. The "Princesse de Caraman-Chimay" bedroom, meanwhile, is a tribute to Jacqueline Hennessy, heir to the cognac firm of that name, who married a descendent of Alfred Werlé. This bedroom features Mathieu Lehanneur's spectacular *Once Upon a Dream,* an installation designed to encourage sleep, in a nod to the insomnia that afflicted Madame Clicquot. The room is a comforting bubble, with "white noise" that shields the sleeper from disturbing sounds. Curtains drawn, the light dims slowly, the temperature is maintained at a perfect 19°C (66°F), while a breath of mineral-laden sea air steeps the cells in its anti-oxidizing, hydrating effects. Tension melts away, the mind unwinds, the body relaxes.

Once the rooms have been assigned, visitors head back downstairs to join their hosts in the grand salon. Above the fireplace, the traditional panel is replaced by a chamfered mirror redesigned by Bruno Moinard. Two Empire console tables inherited from Édouard Werlé's family have been refurbished to mark their entry into this new page of the residence's history.

Finally, it is mealtime. The dining room sparkles with gilding against a spectacular field of mat black and ash-gray parquet flooring. In the middle of the room stands a large table that seats eighteen, ringed by mahogany chairs upholstered in a patchwork of black-and-Clicquot-yellow horsehair. As in a fairy tale, the light comes from a huge chandelier with smoked-glass pendants. If the sunlight is still too harsh, large shiny linen curtains are drawn over the windows.

SUBTLE POWER

In this impressive setting, visitors can sample refined, well thought-out cuisine accompanied by the most stirring of Veuve Clicquot's many paradoxes: the one to be drunk. The major characteristics of Veuve Clicquot champagne are the strength, powerful structure, and rich flavor made possible by a predominance of Pinot Noir grapes.

Dominique Demarville, cellar master at Veuve Clicquot since 2009, is charged with maintaining the Veuve Clicquot style. Each year, he is given five hundred new wines and a large quantity of reserve wine—another of the firm's characteristic strong points—to achieve this goal. These wines come from the company's own vineyards, spread over thirteen plots rated *grand cru* and eighteen plots of *premier cru.* The flagship champagne, Brut Yellow Label, is blended from no fewer than seventy different wines, up to one-third of which will be reserve wines that may have already aged for ten years or more, thereby guaranteeing the steadfastness of the Veuve Clicquot style. Over half of these wines are made from Pinot Noir grapes, which give the house style its delicate fruitiness, structure, and power. The rest of the blend will be fifteen percent to twenty percent Pinot Meunier and roughly thirty percent Chardonnay. Brut Yellow Label is a wine with aromas that first evoke fruit, followed by hints of vanilla, then brioche. In the mouth, its strong attack gently gives way to a well structured roundness and remarkable length, as notes of fruit and spice persist. It is not only perfect as an aperitif, but is also an ideal companion to fish and seafood, indeed to an entire meal.

Veuve Clicquot Rosé, recreated in 2006 (the first pink champagne in history, in 1775, was a Clicquot), was an instant hit and has now become the firm's second mainstay. Its popularity is probably due to its ability, while still young, to

PAGE 106: *Casks and candles are placed in one of the limestone cellars where a bottle of champagne is about to be disgorged. Disgorging involves expelling the yeast deposits that accumulate in the neck of the bottle. This tricky operation was once done by hand by skilled workers.*
PAGE 107: *Carefully archived, bound volumes contain copies of all company correspondence in the days of Édouard Werlé, who headed the company until 1884.*
FACING PAGE: *In the cellars cut from limestone is a legendary stairway marked with the years of great Veuve Clicquot vintages.*

project great freshness and fruity harmonies of raspberry, wild strawberry, cherry, and blackberry, followed swiftly by flavors of dried fruit, apricot, and brioche. The entire experience is structured and elegant, thanks to the dominance of Pinot Noir, as reflected in the champagne's glowing, appealing color. Veuve Clicquot Rosé is a truly great pre-dinner treat.

Veuve Clicquot's vintage wines are beautiful, complex expressions of the house skills and experience. Age further embellishes their structure, making them particularly suited to accompany sophisticated dishes. Vintage Brut—a distant but worthy heir to the first vintage champagne made by Madame Clicquot in 1810—owes its power to the two-thirds proportion of Pinot grapes, and its elegance and freshness to the one-third measure of Chardonnay. This perfect equilibrium makes it particularly appropriate for fish, shellfish, and white meats. Veuve Clicquot also makes a vintage rosé as well as a "dosed" version, Vintage Rich, a dry champagne that chefs like to court for its amazing revelatory potential.

In 2010 Demarville created "Cave Privée," a collection of the rarest and most glamorous vintages of the past several decades. Each numbered bottle is the object of particular disgorging and dosing based on its size and the characteristics of its year. The collection currently includes two vintage bruts—1980 and 1990—and three vintage rosés—1975, 1978, and 1989. This collection is a revelation of the amazing work accomplished by cellar masters and their teams of oenologists over a period of decades.

Finally, in a final tribute to the widow Clicquot, La Grande Dame is the house's most glamorous champagne. Its 1962 vintage was first put on the market in 1972 to celebrate the firm's two hundredth anniversary. It was then packaged in an old-style bottle in very dark glass, which is squat and slightly narrow at the base. A fine ship's anchor and a comet were engraved into the glass as the distinctive symbols of Veuve Clicquot. Composed exclusively of wines aged for a minimum of six years and made from grapes from the finest plots of eight *grand cru* vineyards, La Grande Dame is generous with her silky flavor, finesse, and extremely delicate aromas, which obviously vary from year to year. La Grande Dame Rosé, meanwhile, was born in 1996 from the 1988 vintage. The rich, rare white version was artfully blended with an additional 15 percent red wine from Bouzy made with grapes from the best plots of the vineyard. It brings further complexity expressed as the noble richness of dried fruit such as figs and dates, enlivened by sweet spices such as vanilla. La Grande Dame Rosé is a most unusual wine and should be enjoyed on its own, or in the company of only the most refined foods such as lobster, caviar, or truffles. Powerful and gentle at the same time, it embodies the quintessence of the paradoxical grace of Veuve Clicquot champagne.

Whichever nectar is offered to guests, it will be enhanced by food designed to accompany it. Such dishes have been devised by Veuve Clicquot's house chefs, Laurent Beuve and Christophe Pannetier, who did not wait for the resurrection of the hôtel du Marc (with a complete renovation of the kitchen) to start exploring the gastronomic universe of Veuve Clicquot in collaboration with the firm's oenologists. The company has long received guests for lunch or dinner almost every day of the year, at

Veuve Clicquot Rosé, recreated in 2006 (the first pink champagne in history, in 1775, was a Clicquot), was an instant hit and has now become the firm's second mainstay.

FACING PAGE: *Built in the center of Reims in 1840, the hôtel du Marc is another lavish residence now used to receive guests. Cellar master Dominique Demarville welcomes privileged visitors to highly select tastings.*
Faithful to the spirit of the first pink Clicquot, which dates back to 1775, Veuve Clicquot Rosé was reinvented in 2006 (bottom, left). Its rich notes of fruits, nuts, and brioche make it a wonderful pre-dinner champagne.

THIS MODERNITY, IN CONJUNCTION WITH GREAT ELEGANCE AND TRADITIONAL HERITAGE, HAS BEEN EVIDENT IN THE HÔTEL DU MARC SINCE 2011, AFTER FOUR YEARS OF PATIENT RESTORATION.

PAGES 112–113: *Although steeped in eighteenth-century classicism, since 2011 the hôtel du Marc has been redesigned with resolutely modern interiors by the architect Bruno Moinard. The stylized curves of the ramp at the top of the staircase echo the entwined shafts of wood sculpted by Pablo Reinoso to evoke vinestocks.*

ABOVE AND FACING PAGE: *The new interior design of the hôtel du Marc (here the entrance hall with its fine staircase and screen of narrow strips of mirror) expresses the boldness and creativity displayed by Barbe-Nicole Ponsardin in her own day. Widowed in 1805 while still young, she boldly ran the Clicquot firm, inherited from her husband, all on her own.*

both the hôtel du Marc and the Verzy manor. Some occasions are particularly special, such as the annual gourmet dinner for the Veuve Clicquot Award, and the meals offered—over several days—to the company's two or three hundred suppliers of grapes. These daily visits and events provide an occasion to elaborate dishes that go particularly well with a given champagne. Furthermore, the chefs regularly come up with ideas for their counterparts the world over, in the form of recipes that can be freely adapted far from France.

At Veuve Clicquot, the quest for a perfect match between food and wine follows two major yet distinct principles: either both parties share the same flavors, creating a perfect resonance, or they establish a balance of contrasts. The first approach to culinary combinations means, for example, that sweet will go with sweet, acidic with acidic, spicy with spicy. Thus Vintage Brut 2004, with its lively acidity of fresh citrus and other fruits, is an ideal companion to a salad of lobster with citrus fruit. On the other hand, the right balance of contrasts—salty with sweet, bitter with spicy, or acidic with oily—can be delicious. This kind of contrast is exemplified by accompanying the lightly spicy, mineral flavor of a filet of duckling and root vegetables with a Vintage Rosé 2004, whose initial freshness in the mouth concludes with sweet notes of honey and almond.

Such combinations of flavors also work well with Brut Yellow Label. As mentioned above, its power and finesse, its notes of fruit and spices, have led chefs and wine specialists to favor certain obvious connections: blinis and crackers with duck, salmon, parmesan, and all hard cheeses. The chefs also propose some recipes perfect for hors-d'oeuvres: a brochette of smoked duck breast, banana, and allspice; a brochette of pink grapefruit and sautéed shrimp with vanilla; crab marinated in lime juice, red pepper, and coriander; cheese-filled flaky pastry; dried apricot stuffed with foie gras and sliced almonds. Moving on to main courses, they have come up with herb-roasted goose with tagliatelle, roast duck with baby vegetables, sautéed salmon with baby vegetables and sesame seeds, linguine with sea food, and a salad of red mullet with eggplant caviar. In short, these simple dishes—accessible to all—are delicious companions to one of the most famous champagnes in the world.

"Cave Privée," a collection of the rarest and most glamorous vintages of the past several decades. Each numbered bottle is the object of particular disgorging and dosing based on its size and the characteristics of its year.

FACING PAGE: *A new room in the hôtel du Marc dubbed the Atelier (Workshop) is designed to allow the cellar master to organize tasting sessions with the head chef, who immediately invents gastronomic delights that orchestrate the crescendo of aromas and flavors released by rare Clicquot champagnes. Lucky guests at these special occasions sample and savor these wonderful combinations around a large table of stainless steel and white Corian.*
PAGE 119: *A recent, original recipe by the chef was specially created to go with Brut Yellow Label, whose fruity attack is followed by impressions of vanilla and brioche, blossoming into final notes of fruits and spice.*

Chef Laurent Beuve's Recipe

FLAKED KING CRAB AND AVOCADO TARTAR
WITH SLOW-ROASTED TOMATOES
AND GRANNY SMITH APPLES

INGREDIENTS
Serves 6

· 8 oz. (250 g) king crab flesh
· 1 shallot, finely chopped
· 1 teaspoon curry powder
· A little olive oil
· 3 avocados
· A few sprigs chives
· Juice of 1 lime
· 6 slow-roasted tomatoes
· 1 Granny Smith apple
· 3 slices *viande des Grisons*
  (air-dried beef)
· 2 teaspoons (10 ml) balsamic
  vinegar
· 2 tablespoons (30 ml) olive oil
· 6 oyster leaves
· Salt and freshly ground pepper

METHOD
Combine the crab flesh with the shallot and curry powder. Season with salt and pepper, drizzle with a little olive oil, and chill.
Peel the avocados and cut them into small dice.
Snip the chives and stir carefully into the diced avocado.
Stir in the lime juice and season with salt and pepper.
Cut the tomatoes and apple into julienne slices.
Cut each slice of air-dried beef in half. Dry the slices in a 300°F (150°C) oven for 5 minutes.
Make a vinaigrette dressing with the balsamic vinegar and olive oil.
In each of six 2-inch (5-cm) rings, arrange a layer of avocado, a layer of slow-roasted tomatoes, and crab flesh. Chill.
Place the rings containing the crab in the center of the serving plates and carefully remove them. Add the sliced apple and air-dried meat and garnish with an oyster leaf. Serve well chilled with a drizzle of balsamic vinegar.

Note: Oyster leaves (*Mertensia maritima*) grow wild on the coast of Scotland. They have the appearance of a thick spinach leaf, and a salty flavor.

VEUVE CLICQUOT HAS LONG RECEIVED GUESTS FOR LUNCH OR DINNER ALMOST EVERY DAY OF THE YEAR, AT BOTH THE HÔTEL DU MARC AND THE VERZY MANOR.

ABOVE AND FACING PAGE: *Mat black, ash gray, glossy gray, mahogany, and touches of Clicquot-yellow on the chairs create a thoroughly contemporary elegance within the setting of eighteenth-century woodwork. The refined table setting echoes chef Laurent Beuve's talent for marrying flavors. Young guinea fowl is served with figs, root vegetables, wild-mushroom fricassees, and a thyme sauce that subtly reveal the full range of fruity, spicy aromas found in Veuve Clicquot's famous Brut Yellow Label.*

KRUG

Krug enjoys a very special reputation among true aficionados, who would never swap their favorite champagne for any other brand. They're called "Krug lovers," and they include the likes of Ernest Hemingway, who ritually ordered two bottles of Krug at breakfast when he was living at the Ritz just after the war, according to Marcel Duhamel, his secretary at the time. And then there was Coco Chanel (who would never think of organizing a fashion show unaccompanied by Krug), Maria Callas, Hubert van Karajan, and Yves Montand. They have been succeeded by many of today's celebrities whose names Krug prefers not to cite, out of respect for their privacy.

So what makes Krug so different? It's a small operation, of course, and its "haute couture" approach to champagne produces small yields each year, yet it is present and even venerated all over the planet. The only explanation is the very special sight, smell, and taste of Krug champagnes. The Krug color is unique: an intense gold enlivened by coppery highlights and bubbles of legendary finesse. The Krug bouquet is instantly recognizable—an explosion of enchanting scents of ripe fruit and flowers, which on the palate become a tapestry of warm, sun-drenched, sensuous flavors with a fresh, airy sensation that lasts and lasts, seemingly forever. A single sip persists infinitely.

The company's illustrious history began one fine day in 1843 when Joseph Krug, unhappy with the uneven quality of existing champagnes, decided to establish his own firm. Krug was a passionate, generous, and hedonistic man who knew that champagne could provide a richer experience. He wanted to offer customers a totally new champagne, one they could drink year after year with the same enthusiasm thanks to the wine's outstanding finesse. Krug was born in Mainz, Germany, in 1800, and was the son of a meat merchant who was a local dignitary, then mayor of the city. At the age of twenty-four, Krug decided to cross the border and move permanently to France. For a while he lived in Paris, renting a place that belonged to the family of court painter Élisabeth Louise Vigée-Lebrun. At some point a fellow German recommended Krug to a large champagne merchant at Châlons-sur-Marne, Jacquesson & Fils, where he began as an accountant in 1834. Krug rose rapidly through the ranks, becoming the owner's right-hand man, negotiating directly with banks and shippers, all the while acquiring

knowledge of winemaking from a highly respected wine merchant in Reims, Hippolyte de Vivès. In 1841 Krug married an Englishwoman, Emma Jaunay, his boss's sister-in-law. Krug thus became his employer's brother-in-law (their two wives being sisters), and Emma gave birth to a son, Paul, the following year. Business was booming and Krug seemed to be enjoying the best of all possible worlds. Yet by 1842 Krug decided to abandon his comfortable situation.

We might be able to guess his reasons: after spending eight years in the business, traveling a good deal and comparing wines against one another, he had developed a lofty notion of champagne, and had an idea that he wanted to implement. He became an independent wine merchant, and the following year, in 1843, teamed up with Vivès, who wanted to retire but had no successor. They reached an agreement in the form of a limited partnership, which left Krug in charge of the firm; since French law stipulated that a firm had to be registered under the name of the active partner, the company was officially listed as Krug & Compagnie on November 1, 1843.

Krug started out by pursuing the business of his predecessor, Vivès, buying and selling all kinds of wines, including one fine wine from Bouzy and another from Aÿ. At the same time, thanks to his gift for languages, he was able to prospect foreign markets intensively, establishing deals with firms in England, Germany, Russia, the United States, and Brazil. In 1845, he finally developed his first champagne, and over forty thousand bottles of it were put on the market. In 1846, he began to buy his own grapes, the better to control the entire process of making champagne. The Krug saga had begun.

Since arriving in Champagne, Krug had learned a lot about wine. And he probably possessed a talent that he had always sensed, but had never been able to exercise independently. Whatever the case, the champagne he created, Krug Grande Cuvée, was very different from the others because it transcended the notion of "vintage year." It was an immediate hit. A book on Reims and the surrounding area published as early as 1846 (the year Krug acquired French nationality) mentioned his champagne as being among the best. Thus were born Krug's high standards, whose main features its inventor scrupulously wrote down in 1848 in a small, bright red notebook discovered in an old wooden chest one hundred and twenty-five years later by his great-grandson, Paul Krug II. "You cannot make good wine unless you use the right ingredients and the finest harvests. It is possible to obtain apparently good wine by using average or even poor harvests, but that is an exception that you should never count on; you risk ruining the operation or losing your reputation."

But in fact it was through oral tradition, through the daily life of the firm and the annual cycle of harvests and tastings, that the Krug family has transmitted its terrific skills from father to son for six generations. But skills are just part of a philosophy that includes always trying to transcend current standards, seeking the ultimate pleasure

Krug enjoys a very special reputation among true aficionados. They include the likes of Ernest Hemingway, who ritually ordered two bottles of Krug at breakfast when he was living at the Ritz just after the war, according to Marcel Duhamel, his secretary at the time.

FACING PAGE: *A view of Clos du Mesnil and its outbuildings (top). Krug's exclusive Clos du Mesnil champagne is made solely from Chardonnay grapes hasvested in a single year, planted in this plot of just four and a half acres. Olivier Krug (bottom, left) now represents the sixth generation directly descended from his ancestor, Joseph Krug (bottom, right), who founded the company in 1843 determined to establish the strictest standards for his unique champagne.*

of drinking champagne. The Krug Grande Cuvée being enjoyed in the early third millennium is thus the faithful, steadfast expression of the unique style imagined and elaborated right from the start by Joseph Krug. "If he should ever return among us some day to taste our Krugs," say the family, "he'd be able to say with a big smile, 'That's the very Krug I was looking for.'"

Joseph bequeathed his son Paul a well-established firm with a good reputation in several countries for its highly sought-after champagnes. Paul also inherited his father's great sincerity, taste for authenticity, and aversion to artifice. He also places relentless stress on quality. Paul had worked alongside his father for seven years before taking over the firm, which he acquired outright when Monsieur de Vivès withdrew from the partnership in 1868. To everything his father had taught him, Paul added a sense of perfectionism and a tireless interest in new markets, notably England where he had spent part of his schooling. London soon became Krug's largest outlet. Benefiting from the favorable economic climate, sales rose significantly once the crisis provoked by the phylloxera epidemic had passed. The resulting profits enabled Paul to build a series of cellars and new offices on Rue Coquebert in Reims, where the firm is still headquartered today.

Paul married a woman from Rouen, Caroline Harlé, and the couple had ten children. The eldest, Joseph, took over the company after his father's death in 1910. Born in 1869, Joseph lived for nearly a century, dying in 1967 and making an unforgettable mark in the Champagne region, where his sensitivity, kindness, and enthusiasm for travel, roses, and the sea set him apart from the often-harsh world of the wine business. And he was able to bring courage and intelligence to bear on the crises he had to face—two world wars, a depression, the Russian revolution, American prohibition—which ultimately consolidated Krug's prestige.

Mobilized in 1914, Joseph was taken prisoner and only returned to Reims after the war was over; during those years it was his wife Jeanne, grand-niece of the great lexicographer Pierre Larousse and god-daughter of Victor Hugo, who kept the business going with the help of a few cellar men who hadn't been drafted. In 1915 she even dared to compose a vintage champagne—which enjoyed great success. This vintage 1915 Krug was elaborated largely from grapes near the Montagne de Reims district since the Germans were blocking Côte des Blancs and a lack of transportation during the war made it hard to seek supplies further afield. The vintage was therefore made exclusively from Pinot Noir grapes and had a deep, almost pale claret color. Meanwhile, Reims was being heavily bombarded, and the company cellars on Rue Coquebert were turned into a school and a hospital, as well as a chapel for Protestant religious services. For her devotion to the war effort and her determination to be among the last civilians to evacuate Reims, Jeanne was awarded the Croix de Guerre and dubbed a knight of the Légion d'Honneur.

Thus were born Krug's high standards, whose main features its inventor scrupulously wrote down in 1848 in a small, bright red notebook discovered in an old wooden chest 125 years later by his great-grandson, Paul Krug II.

When Joseph finally returned from prison camp he was gravely ill, and he only slowly assumed his old functions. But he had the thrill of creating, along with his nephew Jean Seydoux who had joined the firm, the vintage Krugs of 1928 and

PAGES 128–129: *The inner courtyard of company headquarters on Rue Coquebert in Reims shortly before World War II. Cases of champagne are ready to be shipped to England, the United States, Brazil, and elsewhere. The layout of the courtyard and buildings remains the same today: on the left is the entrance to the cellars, while the building on the right has been renovated to host guests for tasting sessions.*
FACING PAGE: *The small red notebook in which company founder Joseph Krug scrupulously wrote down the founding principles of the champagne he developed.*

1929, legendary champagnes that left a permanent mark in history. Joseph also continued the task, begun by his predecessors, of continually expanding foreign markets. In the 1930s, over ninety percent of Krug's yield was exported, a figure that was most unusual in Champagne at the time. In England, the house of Krug had the honor of being named official supplier to the court of Saint James during the reign of George V, and has remained so ever since. During World War II, their activities in the French Resistance cost Joseph and Jeanne a spell—two spells, in Jeanne's case—in a Gestapo jail.

Joseph Krug II finally retired in 1958. His son Paul, born in 1912, had joined the family business in 1935. Paul's reign was one of continuity, preserving ancestral skills and traditions such as an initial fermentation in small oak casks. Unlike most other makers of champagne in the 1950s, he pursued these practices in order to monitor the yield of each plot individually (which can no longer be done in large vats that mix different harvests). He also continued to bottle-age his champagnes in the cellar for at least six years. In the 1960s and 1970s, in response to growing demand yet with a concern to maintain the highest standards of quality, Paul sought to guarantee reliable supplies of grapes by buying vineyards in Ville-Dommange, Aÿ, and Le Mesnil-sur-Oger, as well as by signing long-term contracts with specially selected wine growers. These new resources made it possible to avoid a situation that threatened to ruin Krug's relations with his clients. The champagne was in great demand but in short supply and Paul was occasionally unable to completely fill orders from well-known restaurants. Alongside consolidating his supply of fine quality grapes, Paul also sought to consolidate the firm in terms of financing and marketing in the 1970s. When he retired in 1977, his two sons Henri and Rémi (who joined the firm in 1962 and 1965, respectively) were able to

assume the full running of the company. Paul nevertheless continued to participate in tastings and the creation of new vintage champagnes right up to his death in 1997.

Krug enjoys blending wines from highly expressive Pinot Noir and Chardonnay grapes with a palette of specially selected Pinot Meunier wines.

Confident in the company's strong fundamentals yet also aware of the challenges created by the ever-accelerating changes that marked the second half of the twentieth century, Henri and Rémi both sought to build the prestige and reputation of the house of Krug. Henri, the wine and vine specialist, composed all of Krug's champagnes following the departure of Paul; he also invented Krug Rosé, followed by the legendary Krug Clos du Mesnil, which celebrated the renaissance of this exceptional vineyard after its patient restoration. Later, he was behind the launch of another Krug single-varietal champagne, Krug Clos d'Ambonnay. In the cellars, Henri constantly monitored all the details that guaranteed excellence by encouraging a dialogue between tradition and innovation. He successfully cultivated relationships of mutual trust and esteem with the wine growers whose best grapes he transformed into champagne. Despite his retirement in 2002, Henri continues to attend, as did his father, all tasting sessions. The tasting committee is still composed of the cellar master, Eric Lebel, the company oenologists, Henri, Henri's son Olivier, and Rémi.

PAGE 132: *Autumn light on a plot of Pinot Noir grapes. The cellars at company headquarters on Rue Coquebert in Reims.*
PAGE 133: *This is where Krug Grande Cuvée ages for a minimum of six years, while vintage Krugs remain here for at least ten years.*
FACING PAGE: *After the harvest, from fall through spring, cellar master Eric Lebel conducts daily tasting sessions that will determine the precise blend—or assemblage—used in Krug Grande Cuvée and vintage Krugs. In addition to 150 reserve wines, a given year's wines from 250 different plots are tasted, compared, and noted.*

Whereas Henri was Krug's nose and palate, Rémi acted as its voice, ears, and legs. A tireless traveler, he constantly toured the world to spread the Krug word and also to meet the younger generations of champagne lovers and seek out their reactions and expectations. He would then share these impressions with Henri in the privacy of the tasting room. It was Rémi who brought Krug into the advertising age. Head of marketing operations for over thirty-five years, he expanded the Krug universe by exploring and then exploiting operations in Italy, the United States, and Asia. It was Rémi's belief that his bottles of champagne should be treated like people, should be seen as participants in—or witnesses to—special moments. So he put all his energy and enthusiasm into stressing their "presence" and their "voice." He constantly refined Krug's glamour, beauty, and value so that its appeal rose ever higher.

The duo formed by the two brothers was highly unusual in the history of champagne. "Joined at the hip," as it were, by the same culture of excellence and the same unique family dream, they both embodied the house of Krug, each with his own different temperament. They simultaneously combined modesty with passion, authenticity with the gift of glamour, and a crucial respect for the fullness of time with an openness to the changing world.

When Henri retired, Rémi took over as CEO at Krug before himself retiring five years later. The sixth generation is now represented by his nephew, Olivier Krug, who pioneered Krug in Japan and insured its success there. Olivier's all-round skills and experience perpetuate Krug's traditions: he is present on every front, from the vineyards to tasting sessions to international markets. Today he is the house expert, ambassador, and director, insuring that the heritage has been passed on. Krug, whose current president is Margareth Henriquez, a wine enthusiast who likes meeting the wine

growers, also benefits from the formidable resources and opportunities offered by the Moët Hennessy (LVMH) group to which it has belonged since 1999.

A CONSTELLATION IS BORN

Ever since it was invented, one of Krug's strengths has been a constant creativity that never succumbs to passing fashion: Krug remains Krug, whatever the cost! Thus the choice of local wines remains highly personal and subjective at Krug, and is guided by perception of taste alone, keeping in mind the idea that every glass of Krug should be remembered with intense pleasure. Krug enjoys blending wines made from highly expressive Pinot Noir and Chardonnay grapes with a palette of Pinot Meunier wines specially selected for their individual character. The wines are added in small doses to the overall assemblage, or blend of wines, and play a role similar to spices in a gourmet dish, bringing out a rich range of flavors. Right from the first day of the annual grape harvest, cellar master Eric Lebel begins to think about assemblages—a single grape, tasted straight from the vine, already points in a certain direction. During the winter and spring months Lebel and the tasting committee then sample, test, and compare the wines as they become more open and expressive, a process that calls for hundreds of tasting sessions. The wines from two hundred and fifty plots, along with one hundred and fifty wines aged from previous years, are assessed. Thus every year over five thousand tasting notes are drawn up and meticulously recorded in black notebooks.

Equally original is Krug's use of oak casks for the initial fermentation. Krug is one of the few major champagne houses continue to use hand-made Champagne hogsheads containing roughly

FACING PAGE: *Grape-picking time at Clos du Mesnil shortly after it was purchased in 1971. This small vineyard of only four and a half acres in the middle of a village in the Côte des Blancs district has been enclosed by a wall since the seventeenth century. Replanted with Chardonnay, in 1979 it yielded an exclusive champagne, Krug Clos du Mesnil. Grapes of a single variety from a single year, unblended, produce a champagne in very limited quantities. In a special harvesting technique, pickers move up and down in successive "passes," harvesting each vine or bunch only at the very right moment. Each year just ten thousand bottles are made available to eager connoisseurs—but only if weather conditions permit.*

fifty-four gallons, and it is the only one that that uses them for all wines. Not because oak adds any particular quality to the wine (Krug makes champagne, not bordeaux or cognac), but because the smaller casks allow for individual fermentation from each plot. Contrary to popular belief, these pale wines are not aged in oak—but they *are* born in oak. They remain in oak casks for a few weeks after harvest, a brief yet decisive moment when each still wine is free to develop its own individuality and temperament, which is crucial in the composition of an assemblage. These early conditions also increase a wine's potential for aging even as they sublimate its freshness, preparing it to develop small, elegant bubbles.

Krug thus maintains the individuality of specific vineyard plots, an approach that was the source of the indisputable quality of the champagne made by founder Joseph Krug. At a time when all champagne houses were using oak casks, Krug was already making a difference by respecting the qualities specific to each sector of vineyard. And this explains why, over and above the simple respect for tradition, these casks are still found on Krug's Rue Coquebert premises, where they scent the vast cellar. It matters little that this method of fermentation requires infinite care and added costs; for Krug, the house style is priceless. People who have been lucky enough to visit the Rue Coquebert cellars (in addition to the extraordinary library of aged wines, discussed below) are amazed at the impressive number of bottles stored in the caves and galleries hollowed from the chalky stone. Reserves amount to seven or eight years of sales, and guarantee that the champagne will have aged perfectly before it leaves the cellar. Grande Cuvée requires a minimum of six years of aging, while vintage Krugs call for at least ten years. Krug's age-old recipe for making champagne is simple: remain

Contrary to popular belief, these pale wines are not aged in oak—but they are born in oak. They remain in oak casks for a few weeks after harvest, a brief yet decisive moment when each still wine is free to develop its own individuality and temperament, which is crucial in the composition of an assemblage.

patient, listen to what the wine has to say, and let time tease out the full richness of meticulously selected, delicately hand-picked and pressed grapes.

Applying all of these principles to every wine that goes into an assemblage enables Krug to produce a dazzling constellation of champagnes at a range of prices related to exclusiveness, all the while insuring that each one shines with the same intensity and quality. At Krug there is no high end and no low end, but rather a series of great champagnes suited to different occasions and to different preferences. All are born from the same Krug style—a harmonious tension of contrasts, a balance between strength and finesse, between liveliness and length in mouth. They all feature extremely delicate bubbles and wonderful freshness.

Let us begin with Krug's annual masterpiece, the Krug Grande Cuvée. With its tiny bubbles that stimulate yet never shock the palate, delivering a magnificent, lastingly fresh bouquet, this wine can be enjoyed throughout a meal. Its timeless and immediately recognizable taste reconciles opposites:

FACING PAGE: *A vineyard outbuilding with characteristic gable—this is where winemakers used to store their equipment. (bottom, right) At Krug, all picking is done by hand.*

fullness and freshness, strength and finesse, richness and elegance, straightforwardness and complexity. All these seemingly antagonistic features are perfectly wedded together. Some fans stress the way the champagne blossoms in the mouth (apple and apple flowers, almonds, ripe fruit and nuts, frangipane, gingerbread, mild spices, brioche, honey and so on), while others appreciate its freshness (a lively, orchestrated precision of rich, lavish citrus notes). Still others thrill to its roasted attack and its hints of hazelnut and nougat that evolve toward the sweet taste of barley sugar and jellied fruit.

Such richness is the product of a simultaneously skilled and indulgent assemblage of wines from a given year with a suitable selection from over one hundred aged wines in Krug's extraordinary library. A given season's dominant qualities are thus balanced and enhanced by appropriate partners. All these wines, from ten different vintages up to fifteen years old, go into Krug's emblematic bottle. After assemblage, the champagne is aged for at least seven years in the cellar prior to sale. Roughly twenty years are thus required to produce a Grande Cuvée. It is also the only prestigious *cuvée* to be sold in splits, which are perfect for informal or private occasions.

Krug Rosé, produced in limited editions, is not just rare and very different from other pink champagnes, it is also the most non-conformist Krug. The first surprising thing about it is its color—salmon-gold with coral highlights— followed by its amazing roundness and power. Behind its spicy quality there emerge harmonies of berries (raspberries, blueberries, strawberries) followed by hints of honey and citrus fruit, capped by a silken, fruity sensation on the palate. The Krugs thought long and hard before diving into their rosé venture. Joseph was against it, and Paul maintained that position into the 1980s. But his

Krug Rosé is the most non-conformist Krug. The first surprising thing about it is its color—salmon-gold with coral highlights—followed by its amazing roundness and power. Behind its spicy quality there emerge harmonies of berries.

sons Henri and Rémy decided to carry out a secret experiment after the drought of 1976. They selected the most supple and fruity specimens from a rich selection of wines produced from three varieties of grape and numerous vintages. To this assemblage they added a great wine made from Pinot Noir grapes from their exclusive property at Aÿ, briefly fermented "on-the-skins" to produce that very special color and texture. In 1983 a few bottles were brought out for a blind tasting. Paul Krug, still in the dark, thought that a competitor was trying to copy Krug. But Henri spilled the beans—the wine was indeed a true Krug. Convinced and delighted, Paul duly adopted Krug's first pink champagne. Ennobled by five or six years of aging in the cellar, this delicious champagne goes wonderfully with seafood, mildly spiced exotic dishes, desserts of red fruit, and even dark, bitter chocolate.

The Krug universe hosts other wines—vintage champagnes. Produced by an assemblage of wines from three varieties of grape harvest in the same year, a vintage Krug is unique, and is therefore an event. It does not compete with the other champagnes, being neither superior or inferior. It is simply different, because made differently— conditions permitting. Indeed, Krug produced no vintage champagnes in 1986 or 1987, whereas the magnificent 1988 was the object of an unusual

FACING PAGE: *The clean lines of the tasting room on Rue Coquebert, where the cellar master and his five-member tasting committee will craft the assemblage of Krug Rosé, produced in limited editions ever since it was launched in 1983. The high art of assemblage means that wine from a small plot, indeed from a specific section within a plot, will be drawn into a small bottle and individually tasted just like the wines from larger plots.*
PAGE 143: *Time's riches: The Krug cellars on Rue Coquebert where bottles of Krug Grande Cuvée age for a minimum of six years alongside vintage Krugs (ten years) and champagnes from the Krug Collection (aged for twenty to thirty years).*

At Krug, nature expounds and expresses itself through
the Krug winemaking process. Krug's philosophy is to make
only special reserve champagnes called Prestige Cuvées.
There's no hierarchy among the Cuvées, just individual qualities.
Time is important at Krug. Today we are launching vintage 2000,
whose price reflects its rarity. Clos du Mesnil 1999
will not be placed on the market—it didn't measure up.
Vintage champagne is a historical record. Our skills are mainly
passed on orally, so it's important to have a physical trace.
Our profession is one of intuition. Recreating La Grande Cuvée
is a highly intellectually exciting challenge for me. I listen,
I take notes. In July and August, in the midst of the vineyards,
I sense what the year will be like, I listen to what nature is telling
me. Then my opinion is shaped and refined through
tasting after tasting. Finally, intuition takes over.

———————

Éric Lebel

CELLAR MASTER

Tasting notes

VINTAGE: *Krug Clos du Mesnil 2000*
HARVEST: *Luxuriant, perfectly ripe grapes.*
SPECIAL FEATURE: *Made from a single harvest of a single variety—Chardonnay—in a single, walled plot of vines.*
FIRST NOSE: *Aromas of ripe apple, caramel, barley sugar, grapes, honey, acacia, citrus fruit.*
ATTACK IN MOUTH: *Generous, leading to flavors of peach, white flowers, spice cake, honey, zest of orange.*
PERFECT COMBINATIONS: *Lobster, crayfish, king prawns, white fish such as turbot, sole, sea bass; also black truffle.*

decision never before taken in Champagne: Krug 1989 was placed on the market prior to the vintage 1988 in order to allow the latter to mature for an additional three or four years, thereby respecting its inherent aging requirements. Whatever the case, vintage Krugs are cellar-aged for at least ten years prior to going on sale.

The Krug heavens also boast two stars that unleash wild enthusiasm, being thoroughly exclusive champagnes: Krug Clos du Mesnil and Krug Clos d'Ambonnay. These champagnes are made only in certain years and only in limited, numbered editions—around ten thousand bottles of Clos du Mesnil, and three to four thousand bottles of Clos d'Ambonnay—from grapes harvested from a single plot in a single year.

The story began in 1971, when the Krug family bought a few extra vineyards to consolidate their supply of grapes. The family was told of a four-and-a-half acre plot, enclosed by walls since 1698, in the village of Mesnil-sur-Oger in the Côte des Blancs district (which has always been one of Krug's favorite vineyard areas); the land included a fine old farmhouse and outbuildings. The Krugs were immediately seduced; not only by the land, which enjoyed the rank of *grand cru* ("first growth"), but by the gentle, south-eastern slope of that land, and by the sheltered micro-climate of the enclosed plot. The idea took root to transform the outstanding potential of this vineyard into a unique champagne. The outcome was far from certain when the Krugs launched the venture, but everything was done to favor the cultivation of this rare pearl. For example, it would have been relatively easy to replant the entire plot, and then harvest the fruit three years later. But the Krugs' friends and relatives in the Bordeaux region had taught them something crucial: the quality of the great bordeaux wines results from a balance between vines of different ages. Henri Krug therefore drew up a timetable for

In 2007, the firm unveiled another, even rarer gem: Krug Clos d'Ambonnay. It was the fruit of wonderful labor that began in 1995 with the purchase of a plot, planted with Pinot Noir, at the edge of the village of d'Ambonnay on the southeast slope of Montagne de Reims.

staggering the replanting of five mini-plots of Chardonnay vines over a period of years. So it was only in 1979, a full eight years later, that a fine, balanced harvest made it possible to vinify the first Krug Clos du Mesnil. A small vineyard of this size can normally be harvested in one day, but for Clos du Mesnil, the Krugs went to the extreme measure of picking the grapes in successive selective harvests over a number of days, so that each row, indeed, each bunch, would be picked at just the right moment. The wine from this first harvest was not merely harmonious, but the crystalline purity of its Chardonnays was so exceptional that it could be bottled without any further assemblage. Krug Clos du Mesnil 1979 nevertheless received the full Krug treatment and was finally made available to connoisseurs in 1986. Clos du Mesnil 1979 inaugurated a whole series of legendary champagnes which are pure yet refreshing, with melodies of almond, hawthorn, and other white flowers tripping across tongue and palate. They are champagnes that call for meditation and should be drunk on their own, or with a few select dishes that provide just the right setting. Great care should be taken, because a Krug Clos du Mesnil is highly delicate despite its generosity and length in the mouth, so fragile is its airy, almost celestial quality.

PAGES 144–145: *The table is set for lunch for a few special guests at Clos du Mesnil at the end of the harvest season.*
FACING PAGE: *A September day in Clos d'Ambonnay. Arnaud Lallement (bottom, left), the Michelin-starred chef of L'Assiette Champenoise and a second-generation Krug loyalist, has devised a variety of dishes with subtle yet noble textures and tastes that make for a picnic as unique as Krug champagne. Lallement's innovative yet rigorous talent, matched to the individual characters of different Krug champagnes, enables diners to enjoy champagne throughout an entire meal. Lobster, carpaccio of Coutancie beef, and wasabi peas (bottom, right).*

Nearly twenty years later, in 2007, the firm unveiled another, even rarer gem: Krug Clos d'Ambonnay. It was the fruit of wonderful labor that began in 1995 with the purchase of another enclosed plot, this time planted with Pinot Noir and measuring only one and a half acres, at the edge of the village of d'Ambonnay on the southeast slope of Montagne de Reims. This miraculous nugget of a vineyard had been noticed a few years earlier by the Krugs, who regularly bought the wine it produced. Unlike Clos du Mesnil, replanting was not necessary. The work thus primarily entailed refining the way the vines were pruned in order to channel growth and limit yield. But ultimately the challenge was the same: bottling the quintessence of a single variety of grape in a champagne of extreme rarity. No more than four thousand bottles—all numbered—are produced and aged for at least ten years before connoisseurs are allowed to snap them up. Krug Clos d'Ambonnay is made only during good years, when the full potential of the plot's infinite richness is reached. The resulting champagne is a powerful wine of great character and finesse whose rich aromas fill the mouth and then blossom into a bouquet of delightfully fresh sensations.

The classic vintages that Krug places on the market every now and then under the label of "Krug Collection" do not always seek such airiness, however fragrant. All Krugs, of whatever type, age wonderfully if they are stored correctly. And over time, some of them yield new, extraordinary qualities at given stages of their maturation, inviting constant rediscovery. Such rediscovery is not possible, alas, with vintage 1893, of which Krug retains only a single bottle in its cellar, nor with the miraculous 1928, now far too rare; but it remains possible with a few bottles from certain splendid years, which Krug carefully selected and shrewdly set aside in its cellars, knowing full

well what they would become twenty or thirty years later, once refined by time. Vintages 1969, 1973, 1976, 1979, 1981, and 1985 are champagnes still full of freshness yet with powerful, delightful hints of leafy undergrowth, candied fruit, even licorice. These are serene, mysterious champagnes to be savored the way a precious manuscript is studied— the story they tell is wide-ranging, adventurous, Homeric. They, too, should preferably be drunk on their own, although their vigor means that they can accompany food as long as it is authentic and refined.

This idea has been fully grasped by Arnaud Lallement, chef of the two-star restaurant *L'Assiette Champenoise* just outside Reims, who has invented new dishes for every old vintage. The love affair between Krug and this glamorous restaurant has been running for several decades— the founder of *L'Assiette Champenoise*, Arnaud's father Jean-Pierre Lallement, had already made it a "Krug territory." After apprenticeships with Michel Guérard, Roger Vergé, and Alain Chapel, the twenty-one-year-old Arnaud joined his father in Reims in 1996. As his knowledge of Krug champagnes deepened, so did his love of them. Not only for their intrinsic richness, but also for their strength of character. Once Arnaud

Lallement follows a coherent principle when it comes to Krug champagnes. Straightforward wines call for straightforward dishes, while complex wines require a cuisine featuring multiple textures and flavors.

Chef Arnaud Lallement's Recipe

FIG AND RASPBERRIES

INGREDIENTS

Serves 8

Linzer Pastry:
- I ½ cups (6 oz./180 g) all-purpose flour
- ⅓ cup (40 g) confectioners' sugar
- I stick plus 3 tablespoons (6 oz./170 g) butter
- 2 egg yolks (40 g)
- Generous ⅓ cup (I oz./30 g) ground almonds
- Small pinch salt

Fig Mousse:
- 12 oz. (350 g) pureed figs
- 3 sheets (6 g) gelatin
- I cup (250 ml) heavy cream, whipped

Fig Jelly:
- 2 cups (500 ml) pureed figs
- 5 sheets (10 g) gelatin

Hazelnut-Pistachio Tuile Cookies:
- 3 tablespoons (40 g) butter
- Scant ½ cup (3 oz./90 g) light brown sugar
- I cup plus 2 tablespoons (270 ml) cold water
- ¼ cup (2 oz./55 g) hazelnuts
- I ½ tablespoons (20 g) shelled pistachios
- I cup plus 2 tablespoons (5 oz./150 g) flour
- ¼ teaspoon (I g) baking powder
- Small pinch (0.5 g) salt

Fig Sorbet:
- I lb. (500 g) pureed figs
- 2 tablespoons (I oz./25 g) sugar
- 2 cups (500 ml) water
- 3 g (¹⁄₁₆ oz.) stabilizer

Fig-Raspberry Emulsion:
- I cup (250 ml) raspberry juice
- 8 oz. (250 g) pureed figs
- I ¼ teaspoons (5 g) sugar
- 5 g (⅛ oz.) soy lecithin
- About 40 raspberries for decoration

METHOD

Linzer Pastry: Rub the flour, confectioners' sugar, and butter together to form crumbs. Mix in the egg yolks, ground almonds, and salt. Chill. With a laminator, roll out to just under ⅛ inch (3 mm) thick. Cut it into 3-inch (8-cm) squares. Bake for 12 minutes in a 350°F (170°C) oven.

Fig Mousse: Soften the gelatin sheets in cold water. Squeeze out the water. Heat some of the pureed figs and stir in the drained gelatin sheets until dissolved. Pour in the remaining puree to cool. Fold in the whipped cream. Pour the mixture into a silicon mold. Cut into 3-inch (8-cm) squares.

Fig Jelly: Soften the gelatin sheets in cold water. Squeeze out the water. Heat some of the pureed figs and stir in the drained gelatin sheets until dissolved. Stir in the remaining puree. Pour the mixture into a silicon mold. Chill until set. Cut into ¾-inch (1.5-cm) squares.

Hazelnut-Pistachio Tuile Cookies: Melt the butter and stir in the sugar. Pour in the water to cool. Add the hazelnuts and pistachios and chill for 30 minutes. Combine the mixture with the flour, baking powder, and salt. Place in an airtight container and freeze. Slice with a meat slicer (thickness 2). Arrange on a baking sheet and bake for 10 minutes at 350°F (170°C).

Fig Sorbet: Make a syrup with the water, sugar, and stabilizer. Stir it into the pureed figs and process in an ice-cream maker.

Fig-Raspberry Emulsion: Heat the raspberry juice and pureed figs gently. Add the other ingredients and process.

To Plate: In the center of the plate, place a square of Linzer pastry. Top it with a cube of fig mousse. Make an oval scoop of fig sorbet and place it in the center.
Surround with cubes of fig jelly, about five per plate, and about five fresh raspberries.
Process the fig-raspberry emulsion, skim off the foam, and place it over the scoop of sorbet.

became head of the restaurant three years later, he began developing a "made-to-measure" cuisine for his favorite champagne. His menu sets an unmistakable tone right from the start: Krug is drunk by the glass as an aperitif.

Lallement follows a coherent principle when it comes to Krug champagnes. Straightforward wines call for straightforward dishes, while complex wines require a cuisine featuring multiple textures and flavors. This principle can be adopted by everyone at home when enjoying Krug with a meal. In fact the hierarchy of champagnes that certain chefs establish does not at all suit the Krug philosophy, and has been radically banished here. To accompany a rare Krug Clos du Mesnil—a blanc de blanc made from a single plot of vines, and whose strong point is therefore its purity—nothing will do so well as a single yet highly refined product whose authenticity the chef will underscore not through artifice but by drawing out subtle, Baudelairean correspondences between, say, the color white and the striking clarity of a vegetal flavor by preparing a first course of gnocchi simply seasoned with grated white Alba truffles to accompany a Krug Clos du Mesnil. Lallement follows the same principle with an even rarer Krug Clos d'Ambonnay, a blanc de noirs also made from a single plot of vines, whose powerful, supple yet fleshy impact is best appreciated in winter, when it can echo noble black truffle with its vibrant notes of earth and peat, grated over a lightly grilled sliced of home-made bread.

On the scale of increasing complexity, next come the vintage Krugs, wines made from a single year's harvest of grapes of different varieties and plots, which go well with dishes that are not overly sophisticated yet play on complementary textures and flavors. For instance, to accompany a vintage

1998 Krug Lallemant came up with turbot well grilled on the outside but still creamy inside, accompanied by a sauce made with a *vin jaune*. The *vin jaune* sauce could hardly be wed with any wine other than the Krug.

The greatest difficulty comes with Krug Grande Cuvée, assembled from a hundred wines of different varieties and years, some of them fifteen years old. This complex assemblage calls for a baroque dish such as a "pigeon tower" built in layers—a layer of spinach followed by a layer of tomatoes, then a layer of pigeon, followed by a layer of peas, and so on. The same game is played with Krug Rosé, which the chef likes to match to desserts made from fruit such as apple or pear.

Let us return to the Krug Collection, those old vintage champagnes that open like a library of long-forgotten scents and flavors after a lost key has been found. Each tasting is a surprise, especially since a vintage 1964 or 1973, enjoyed just three months ago, will no longer be the same in three years. So Lallement, in conjunction with his customers, likes to improvise on the spot: only after the bottle has been opened and tasted will he compose an original culinary creation inspired what his nose and mouth tell him. Yet that inspiration, like all true artistry, will also stem from one intangible factor: an instantly recognizable style. And thanks to delectable encounters day after day for more a decade, the styles of chef Arnaud Lallement and Krug champagne meet and marry spontaneously.

Lallement's menu sets an unmistakable tone from the start: Krug is drunk by the glass as an aperitif.

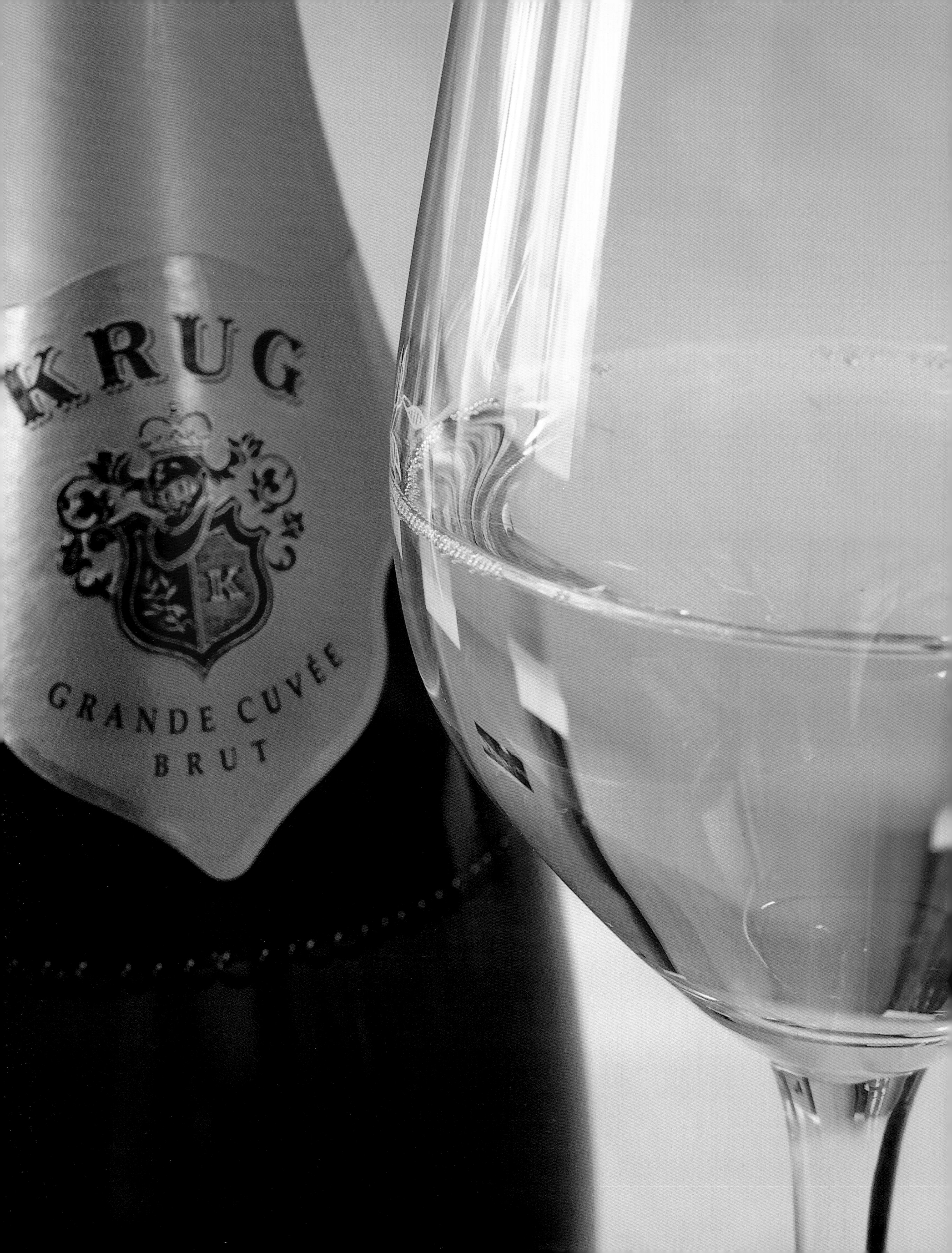
KRUG
GRANDE CUVÉE
BRUT

RUINART

A Benedictine monk, Dom Thierry Ruinart, inspired the birth of the glamorous champagne house that bears his name. Founded in 1729, it is the oldest house of all. Despite the turbulence of what is almost three centuries of history, the monk invites us to appreciate its silence once more. Whereas the silence of the abbey of Hautvillers, where Dom Thierry Ruinart died, is interrupted by nature's song, the Ruinart house in Reims enjoys absolute silence. Its intensity can be experienced when visiting the chalk caves that have served as wine cellars since 1770. Many champagne producers own such chalk pits, but the twenty-four caves here, listed as a historic monument in 1931, are among the most beautiful. Their beauty resides in their surprises; their labyrinthine corridors meander and intertwine one hundred feet below ground level; there is a surprise in store at every turn in the narrow passageways; at the bottom of a hidden stairway, an enormous cathedral-like space or a honeycombed gallery may appear, suddenly illuminated in the dancing light of sodium lamps. These impressive grottoes were quarried from the Gallo-Roman era up to the sixteenth century in order to extract soft chalk that hardened on contact with the air and could be used as building material. Deeper down, the chalk becomes harder, hence more solid, so the quarrymen were able to progressively widen the cave as they dug, carving out a shape that curiously resembles a champagne bottle.

Sheltered from light and vibrations in a constant temperature of 50°F (11°C), these chalk pits seemed to Claude Ruinart, the son of the founder, an ideal spot for maturing wines. So Claude bought the caves beneath Butte du Moulin de la Housse from the city, along with the surface land where he soon erected buildings. During World War I, the caves served as shelters from German bombardments and school lessons were given there. André Ruinart even installed his offices in the grottoes during the war years. But the atmosphere of the caves, however well suited to wine, is not conducive to a long stay by human beings. Sadly, André Ruinart contracted tuberculosis there, and in 1919 he died. The subterranean darkness of the chalk pits had also experienced previous incarnations, having served as secret pagan temples in the early days of Christianity and as underground passages for medieval merchants seeking to smuggle their wares past local tollhouses.

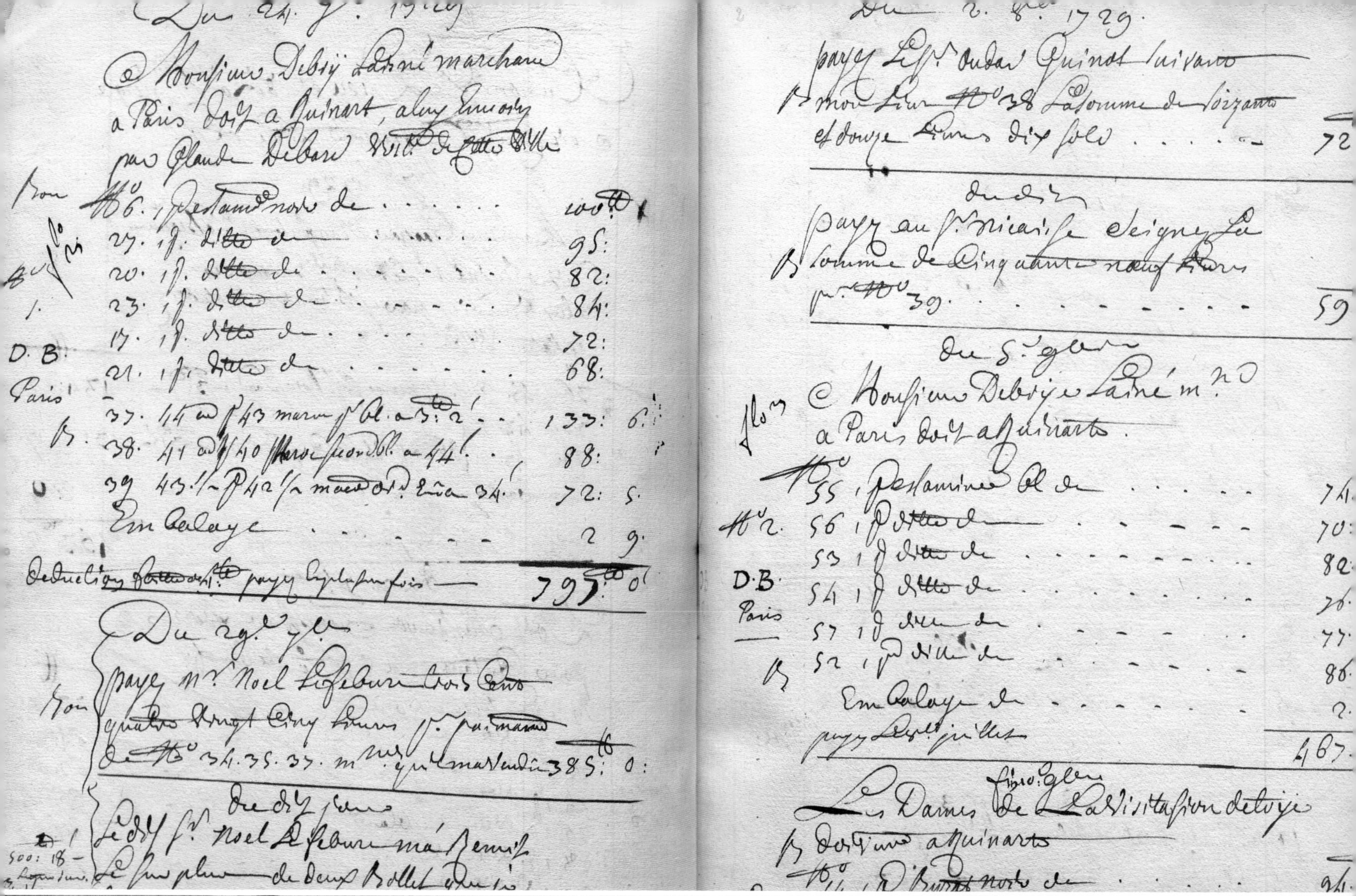

Left page

Du 24. 7bre 1729

Monsieur Debsij l'ainé marchand
a Paris doit a Quinart, alloy Envoyé
par Claude Debart Wit de Latte St Vie

Bon	N° 6.	1	Peste anne noire de	. . . . .	100₶
	27.	19.	d°tte de	. . . . .	95:
B.	20.	19.	d°tte de	. . . . .	82:
1.	23.	19.	d°tte de	. . . . .	84:
D.B	17.	19.	d°tte de	. . . . .	72:
	21.	19.	d°tte de	. . . . .	68:
Paris	37.	44 d° P 43 marw p° Bl a 3: 2		. .	133: 6:
B.	38.	41 d° P 40 Arvs second Bl a 44		.	88:
C.	39	43½ P 42½ maw d° Enu 34		.	72: 5.
		Em Calaye	. . .	. . .	2 9.

Deduction pour avoir payé le plus en fois ————— 799:00

Du 29.e 7bre

payé Mr Noel Lefebure trois Cens
quatre vingt cinq Livres p° pai maen°
de N° 34. 35. 37. m mes quil m'a vendu 385: 0:

Du dix Juin
le dit Sr Noel Lefebure m'a Remis
500: 18   de Surplus de deux Bollet de ..

Right page

Du 2. 8bre 1729.

payé le Sr Oudart Quinot suivant
mon livre N° 38 La somme de soizante
et douze Livres dix sols . . . . . . — 72

Du d°
payé au Sr Nicaise Seigney la
somme de Cinquante neuf Livres
p° N° 39 . . . . — 59

Du S.t glen

Monsieur Debsije l'ainé m N°
a Paris doit a Quinart.

N°°	55	1	Peste anne Bl de	. . . . .	74
N° 2.	56	1	d°tte de	. . . . .	70
	53	19	d°tte de	. . . . .	82
D.B	54	19	d°tte de	. . . . .	70.
Paris	57	19	d°ue de	. . . . .	77
B.	52	19	d°ue de	. . . . .	88
		Em Calaye de	. . . . .	. .	2
		payé le 21 Juillet			467

Les Dames de La Visitation de Voije
p doit une a Quinart

N° | 19 | A° Burre noire de | . . . . | 94

Centuries of secrecy and mystery invest these galleries, epitomized by the marks of Gallo-Roman pickaxes and small niches in the wall for holding oil lamps. Nowadays, these vast naves of chalk are filled only with bottles, and silence. An immaculate, absolute silence fills a space so vast and high that shadows mask walls and ceiling. There the silence provides a perfect metaphor for the champagne it nurtures: it evokes the purity, uncompromising rigor, and timelessness of what is known as "the Ruinart flavor."

It has taken several centuries for Ruinart to arrive where it is today. But the firm seemed predestined to succeed, thanks to the chance intervention of one man without whom it might never have existed. Son of a prosperous cloth merchant in Reims, the Benedictine monk Dom Thierry Ruinart was born in 1657 and, at a young age, his abilities caught the eye of one of the greatest historians of the day, Dom Jean Mabillon, who summoned him to the abbey of Saint-Germain-des-Prés in Paris. There, Ruinart became an unusually fine scholar, writing numerous books on religious history and corresponding with the best minds of his generation. These efforts did not prevent him from taking a close interest in the vineyards of his native Champagne region, or in the work of his fellow monk, Dom Pierre Pérignon, with whom he often met. According to the family's own history, Dom Thierry told his brother Nicolas, who was a cloth merchant in Reims like their father, of the commercial potential of a "sparkling wine" which was being developed at Hautvillers and in the region, and which was bringing wealth to local producers. As a sign of the ultimate destiny of his name, Ruinart died in the abbey of Hautvillers in 1709. He had stopped there on his way to Reims, while Dom Pierre was still cellar master. The two monks now lie not far from one another in the abbey church itself, a symbol of the prestige they earned during their lifetime.

Although Nicolas Ruinart paid little heed to his brother's advice, his own son Nicolas, born in 1697, took it to heart. Perhaps he had been spurred by a royal decree, issued by Louis XV in 1728, authorizing the sale and transportation of wine in bottles. It was this decree that finally enabled champagne to take off. So on September 1, 1729, the newly married Nicolas founded his business and began his first account book with the follow words: "In the name of God and the Holy Virgin, may this book commence." Nicolas began shipping wines alongside his traditional business in fabrics. Six years later, the Ruinart firm was no longer selling cloth. Three thousand bottles of Champagne wine were shipped two years after the business started up, a figure that increased ten-fold in the next thirty years. Ruinart's markets were already extensive, including not only Paris and England (from 1752 onward) but especially other large northern European towns in France, Germany, and Flanders. The first Russian client, Prince Repnin, general to Catherine the Great, took delivery of several basket-loads of bottles in Saint Petersburg in 1765. By that time, Ruinart wines were already appreciated throughout Europe by many wealthy burghers, clergy, and aristocrats. The account books include many such entries, for example, for the prince de Ligne, then living in Brussels.

Owning only a few plots of vine plants himself, Nicolas bought grapes from the districts of Saint-Thierry and Montagne de Reims, as well as the Vallée de la Marne, which he vinified in his own

A Benedictine monk, Dom Thierry Ruinart, inspired the birth of the glamorous champagne house that bears his name. Founded in 1729, it is the oldest house of all.

FACING PAGE: *According to family lore, it was the Benedictine monk Dom Thierry Ruinart (bottom, left) who, in conjunction with Dom Pierre Pérignon at the abbey of Hautvillers, convinced his family to embark on the trade in "sparkling wine" that was then emerging in the Champagne region. And it was the monk's nephew, Nicolas Ruinart, who founded the company. The first account ledger (top and bottom, right) bears the date of September 1, 1729, making Ruinart the world's oldest house of champagne.*

barrels. Only part of his wines were actually made into champagne. His son Claude, born in 1731, inherited a flourishing business that he continued to build through tireless travels across Europe to expand the firm's markets. Already wealthy, Claude's clients included Europe's top aristocracy—such as the Cardinal Prince de Rohan, the Prince of Wales (the future George IV), the Prussian crown prince (son of Frederick II), Count Potocki, and Prince Esterházy. Above all, Claude Ruinart de Brimont triumphed by providing his business with the space it needed: he bought the chalk pits on Butte du Moulin de la Housse and erected large buildings over them, in the form of cavalry barracks. On his death in 1798, Claude was succeeded by his son François Irénée. A great traveler like his father, married to a young Norman woman of Irish stock, and speaking several languages, François Irénée continued the firm's conquest of Europe, notably England. Back in Reims, his substantial viticultural and oenological knowledge enabled him to carry out a policy of quality improvement, steadily abandoning wines of mediocre quality and concentrating on the finest growths from the districts of Montagne de Reims and Côte des Blancs. Although he was a staunch monarchist, François Irénée prospered under the French Consulate and Empire as supplier to clients such the Bonaparte family when Napoleon was still First Consul. By 1806 Ruinart was also supplying the likes of Empress Joséphine, Talleyrand, and the marshals whom the emperor had named princes and kings. The fall of Napoleon and the restoration of the French monarchy enabled François Irénée to pursue a brilliant political career. Elected representative for the Marne in 1815, he became mayor of Reims six years later. In 1817, Louis XVIII granted him letters of nobility and a coat of arms, still seen today on the label. François Irénée enjoyed his finest hour in 1825, when as mayor of Reims he officially received Charles X who had

come to be crowned in Reims cathedral. During the celebrations the king made François Irénée a vicomte and named him officer of the Légion d'Honneur. But after the fall of Charles X in 1830 he retired from public life and spent most of his time in the magnificent château he had built at Brimont, enjoying his substantial fortune by peacefully cultivating his vast properties in the Marne region.

The first Russian client, Prince Repnin, general to Catherine the Great, took delivery of several basket-loads of bottles in Saint Petersburg in 1765.

One of his ten children, Edmond, had already taken over the running of the business in 1826. Edmond was the first Ruinart to travel to Russia, in 1827, as well as the first, four years later, to cross the Atlantic and explore the American market. Edmond's son Edgar also traveled to Russia, but concentrated on the English market. Edgar had married an Englishwoman, and it was in England that the childless couple adopted a little orphan girl in a convent. Edgar's stint at the head of the house coincided with the economic boom of France's Second Empire. In 1874, Ruinart also became Supplier to the Court of His Majesty the King of the Belgians. On Edgar's death in 1881, his brother Charles inherited the firm, while his adopted daughter inherited his personal fortune. Charles was the man who truly opened the United States to Ruinart by hiring a dynamic agent, Roosevelt & Schuyler. (The Roosevelt in question was the uncle of Theodore Roosevelt, future President of the U.S.) In 1888 Charles, more attracted by Parisian life, handed over the reins of

FACING PAGE: *Ever since the 1930s it has been a Ruinart tradition to invite special guests to the privacy of the chalk cellars for privileged wine tastings. The mineral purity of the setting incarnates the purity associated with the "taste of Ruinart."*

the company to his son André, then twenty-seven years old.

André Ruinart de Brimont had just married the beautiful Charlotte Riboldi, who was none other than his uncle Edgar's adopted daughter. André was the firm's first modern manager, implementing a dynamic marketing policy to reverse the falling sales of previous years. He considerably strengthened Ruinart's presence on foreign markets by extending his web of representatives and by founding the first Ruinart subsidiary, or "branch house," in England. At the same time, André and his cellar master, Maurice Hazart, set about the task of producing champagnes of truly exceptional quality. In 1898 Ruinart became Supplier to the Court of Bavaria and in 1904 it was named Supplier to the Royal House of Spain. Ruinart's renown was ultimately guaranteed through innovative advertising strategies: as early as 1895, André commissioned Czech artist Alphonse Mucha, one of the most fashionable poster designers then working in Paris, to produce a poster in the art nouveau style for Ruinart; in 1906, André announced a prize of 12,500 francs, called the Ruinart Père & Fils award, to the first person to cross the English Channel in an airplane. French aviator Louis Blériot apparently declined the prize after his successful attempt in 1909, as the award went to the second flyer to accomplish the exploit, in May 1910, namely Jacques de Lesseps, son of the engineer who designed the Suez Canal. The name of Ruinart became a familiar one in the world of sport and in the press, and began to appear on the streets of major capitals as well as emblazoned on assorted daily objects, a strategy that today would be termed merchandizing.

This growth was brought to a brutal halt by the war. Bombardments destroyed company headquarters, and the entire administrative staff, including the boss, transferred their offices to the chalk pits. Ill and exhausted, André died the year after the war finally came to an end. His son Gérard was only seventeen years old at the time, so it was Charlotte, Vicomtesse Ruinart de Brimont, who became the first female head of a major champagne house since that other famous widow, Veuve Clicquot. Charlotte took charge of rebuilding the administrative offices exactly as they had been and, most importantly, of reconquering lost markets. By the time Charlotte died in 1925, the young Gérard inherited a firm that had become prosperous once again, exploiting a brand name known throughout the world. Champagne flowed freely during the Roaring Twenties, and it was Ruinart corks that were popped in chic Paris restaurants such as Maxim's, Le Pré Catalan, and Fouquet's, and in grand hotels like the Crillon and Le Meurice.

Gérard then had to deal with two difficult periods: the depression (Wall Street's "Black Thursday" occurred the same year as Ruinart's bicentenary), and World War II. Throughout this time, he was assisted by a cousin, Bertrand Mure, and a brilliant general manager, Jean-Max Leroy. At the end of the war, in order to enable the firm to start afresh on a new footing, Gérard sold to the company all the land, buildings, and facilities on rue des Crayères, which were still owned by the family. Since extremely costly renovation work was required, Mure turned to a friend, Baron Philippe de Rothschild, the enthusiastic owner of the Mouton Rothschild estate and the creator of Mouton Cadet wine. Rothschild agreed to buy

In 1906, André Ruinart announced a prize of 12,500 francs, called the Ruinart Père & Fils award, to the first person to cross the English Channel in an airplane.

a 50 percent stake in Ruinart, and the company was able to expand. A few years later, however, in 1963, Rothschild left the firm, after failing to replicate the success he had had with his Mouton Cadet.

Mure had to find a new partner. Enter Moët & Chandon, then headed by Robert-Jean de Vogüé. The sale of Ruinart to the number one champagne producer led to the departure of Gérard Ruinart de Brimont, the last head of the house to carry the name of Ruinart. Vogüé took over as CEO, retaining Mure as general manager. The two men had several points in common, including a shrewd sense of public relations. Back in the 1950s Mure had already organized events in the chalk cellars involving celebrities of the day, such as Michèle Morgan, Sophia Loren, Jean Marais, and Fernandel. In the 1960s and '70s the famous Ruinart cellars were visited by the likes of Brigitte Bardot, Philippe Noiret, and Gérard Dépardieu. Vogüé and Mure implemented policies that permitted Ruinart to reinforce its image and its prestige. Alongside Moët & Chandon, one of the world's most famous champagne, Ruinart had to make its mark as a rare, superior champagne destined for the most demanding of connoisseurs. It was in this spirit that Dom Ruinart was created in 1959. The magnificent Dom Ruinart is a complex blend of fine wines made mostly of Chardonnay grapes, marketed in a long-necked bottle with a shape symbolizing Ruinart's venerable history. Its commercial success guaranteed Ruinart's revival. Mure took over from Vogüé as CEO of the firm in 1970, and the following year Vogüé himself was named head of the champagne division of the brand new Moët Hennessy corporation. Mure continued to reinforce Ruinart's reputation right up to his retirement by founding, in 1979, the Ruinart Trophy, an exceptionally successful competition for young sommeliers in France, which was extended to the whole of Europe in 1988, drawing hundreds of young professional sommeliers from some thirty different countries.

When Mure retired in 1981 he was succeeded by Yves Bénard, a local man who already worked for Moët & Chandon, and who was a highly influential figure in the world of champagne. Bénard's efforts focused above all on the quality of the wines and Ruinart's expansion into foreign markets.

THE DEMANDS OF PURITY

The unmistakable "taste of Ruinart" is due to one of its cellar masters, Jean-François Barot. The final fifteen years of the twentieth century witnessed the birth of a range of six Ruinart champagnes which connoisseurs in France and abroad enjoy wrangling over. Their passionate enthusiasm for the "Ruinart flavor" is probably the result of its emphasis on purity and its quest for the absolute. There are not many champagne houses that can boast a coherent range of champagnes with such a distinctive style, based on the same demanding criteria scrupulously followed by Barot's successors.

Firstly, there is an emphasis on purity, achieved by aiming for a natural wine with extremely low amounts of added sugar and no additive of any sort, eschewing anything that might seem alien to the grapes themselves. Brut is the only variety of champagne produced by Ruinart. Secondly, the quest for the absolute is expressed through the elaboration of the qualities of the rarest and most expensive variety of grape used in champagne, the only white variety: Chardonnay. Few champagne houses bow so deferentially before this prince of grapes, because few know how to exploit its two main characteristics, finesse and elegance, which the chalky, mineral soil of Champagne prevents, unlike other winegrowing soils, from evolving toward a "woody" flavor. Ruinart's wines are neither heavy nor thick. Even when very old, and endowed with fine structure and great

Cellar masters enjoy a global grasp of their work,
from the vineyard to the grapes right up to the consumer,
which is something rare in today's professional world.
So we're able to make adjustments throughout the entire
winemaking process, in order to offer consumers a wine that
meets their expectations. That's one of the great satisfactions
of this job: the feeling of work well done, which results in a
seductive champagne that spurs the imagination and makes people
happy. The world of champagne is full of passionate people, from
the ones who work the vineyards to the ones who buy and drink
our champagne. It is such a joy. You might think our job is always
the same, but it's exactly the opposite. Nothing is ever exactly
the same, you learn all the time, with every grape harvest.
Over the years, I find I'm evolving toward better balance,
greater accuracy, subtle intensity. The important thing for
a cellar master is to find a house that feels like *his*.

———

Frédéric Panaïotis
CELLAR MASTER

Tasting notes

VINTAGE: "R" de Ruinart 2006
HARVEST: Two weeks of sun and heat in September hastened ripening. Abundant harvest, picked over a period ranging from September 7 to 25.
ASSEMBLAGE: 52 percent Chardonnay — 48 percent Pinot Noir, all harvested from grand and premier crus in Côte des Blancs and Montagne de Reims.
DOSAGE: 6 grams per liter
FIRST NOSE: Notes of white flowers such as lime leaf and honeysuckle, plus citrus fruit such as bergamot orange and lemon.
ATTACK IN MOUTH: Full and handsomely structured, evolving toward a firm yet lively finale.
PERFECT COMBINATIONS: Scallops, crayfish, and cooked oysters.

aromatic complexity, their freshness stands out, sharp and fine. The marriage of aromatic intensity with lightness in the mouth is a great Ruinart characteristic of which the house is justly proud.

The quintessence of such rigor is found in Dom Ruinart, a vintage champagne that is therefore not made every year. Dom Ruinart is one of Ruinart's Blanc de Blancs, an exclusive blend of grand Chardonnay wines from a single year. The proportion between Chardonnays from Côte des Blancs (roughly 60 percent), with their great aromatic finesse, and those from Montagne de Reims (roughly 40 percent), with their structure and power, is unique among champagnes. This ratio explains the extraordinary impression of plenitude on tasting Dom Ruinart. The fresh tang of exotic fruit and a long-lasting, amazingly mineral quality give it the feel of an old white burgundy. Dom Ruinart is aged for ten years before being placed on the market, and it can be stored for many years more, because one of the characteristics of Chardonnay is that it ages magnificently. The best way to appreciate it is within the silence of the chalk cellars, but a carpaccio of scallops with vanilla oil also does wonders for its finesse, while caviar enhances its mineral qualities. Fabrice Brunet, chef of the culinary lab at the famous Paris caterer Lenôtre, paired salty strips of sea urchins with the stony intensity of Dom Ruinart 2002. Older vintages of Dom Ruinart are perfectly suited to more unctuous dishes such as the porcini risotto that Alain Senderens recommended as a partner to a Dom Ruinart 1990.

A pink version of vintage Dom Ruinart also exists. This rosé is an astonishing, infinitely rich wine. Its high proportion of Chardonnay (over 80 percent) practically makes it a Blanc de Blancs, which is tinted with Pinot Noir red wine. Its spectacular orange hue is produced by the Chardonnay's yellow-green color, and its aromas resemble a great red burgundy, a Volnay, for example. But no other still wine of less than fifteen

Champagne flowed freely during the Roaring Twenties, and it was Ruinart corks that were popped in chic Paris restaurants such as Maxim's, Le Pré Catalan, and Fouquet's, and in grand hotels like the Crillon and Le Meurice.

years old could be so refreshing on the palate. The freshness persists through the rising notes of dried flowers, spices, candied fruit, and licorice as the champagne warms in the mouth. This wine is suited to exotic dishes, to fowl such as pheasant, and to mild spices such as ginger. The cellar master since 2007, Frédéric Panaïotis, advocates dishes that weave a perfect harmony with Dom Ruinart Rosé, such as farm-raised veal with fricassee of mushrooms, roasted lamb with fresh thyme and Colonnata-roasted potatoes, and pigeon (or duck breast) with candied kumquats and semolina with tangerine oil. After a meal, the generosity of pink Dom Ruinart means it can be savored like cognac, quietly, among friends, so that its nose can be fully appreciated (especially if poured into a wine glass rather than a champagne flute). It is therefore hardly surprising that it is also venerated by gourmet cigar smokers who, delighted to have found a suitable champagne that is not a priceless treasure, enjoy it with a light havana.

In France, Ruinart markets a third vintage champagne, which is a more complex, more mineral incarnation of the house's flagship champagne, "R" de Ruinart. Non-vintage "R" de Ruinart is composed of at least 40 percent Chardonnay grapes, and displays the pure aromas of the house style, with the grace of barely ripe fruit fresh from the tree, such as peaches, apricots, and almonds.

PAGE 167: *The cellar master must fulfill the demanding requirement of reproducing the "taste of Ruinart" crafted by his predecessors. He remains faithful to the spirit of a range of six Ruinart champagnes as redefined in the 1990s, to honor the noble personality of one grape variety in particular, Chardonnay. The family coat of arms, conferred by Louis XVIII, is seen in filigree on tasting glasses and on bottle labels.*
FACING PAGE: *A hundred feet below ground, one of the ninety chalk chambers lit by sodium lamps, part of a maze of galleries carved into the soft limestone dating back as early as Roman times. These are the oldest, and probably the most startling, wine cellars in Reims. They have been listed as an historic monument since 1931.*

"R" de Ruinart is a clean, honest, dry champagne, which delivers the purity of its flavor with great lightness and delicacy. Cellar Master Panaïotis recommends dishes with subtle flavors such as white fish—say a brochette of monkfish with wild rice and baby vegetables—or sweetbreads with tarragon or even a more festive vol-au-vent with mushrooms and duck foie gras. In the vintage version of "R" de Ruinart, Pinot Noir grapes deliver stronger sensations than the non-vintage champagne without undermining all the elegance and finesse. A champagne for celebrations or for grand occasions, ideal as an aperitif, it also has admirable length and can serve as a perfect accompaniment to a meal such as baked oysters or a fricassee of scallops.

As the third millennium approached, Roland de Calonne felt that the world's oldest house of champagne could use an injection of vitality, without renouncing any of its venerable principles. Ruinart seemed a little cut off from younger generations, who were intimidated by its apparently distant glamour. Barot thus undertook a bold creation that was designed to refresh Ruinart's image without tarnishing it, and in 1997 the first Ruinart Rosé hit the market. Even today its fruity sweetness is surprising, dominated as it is by hints of cherry, raspberry, and wild strawberry, combined with all the freshness associated with Chardonnay (an unusually high 45 percent for a non-vintage pink champagne). The pure "Ruinart flavor" thus remains intact. The contrast between the wine's fresh liveliness and its delicate, pale pink color conveys the specificity of Ruinart Rosé. Its popularity was also partly due to the shape of the bottle, based on the old bottles with a slightly narrowed base, as seen in still-life paintings from the past. It can be enjoyed throughout a meal, wedded to wide range of straightforward yet subtly textured dishes—Panaïotis suggests as a first course a tartar of fresh salmon or tuna with an arugula salad, followed by

The final fifteen years of the twentieth century witnessed the birth of a range of six Ruinart champagnes. The passionate enthusiasm of the connoisseurs for the "Ruinart flavor" is probably the result of its emphasis on purity.

breast of duckling with mild spices, and rounded off by a dessert medley of raspberry-almond finger and cherry sorbet in a soup of red berries enlivened by balsamic vinegar.

So successful was Ruinart Rosé that the company repeated the gamble four years later, with Ruinart Blanc de Blancs. It was an even greater hit, to the extent of becoming the firm's flagship. This new version of Blanc de Blancs, also bottled in an old-fashioned bottle, expresses purity and simplicity in naturally white, floral notes of hyacinth and hawthorn or fruity overtones of peach and pear. Like all Ruinart champagnes, it has exceptional length in the mouth. And like its older sister, the Rosé, it is to be drunk among friends on all occasions, as an aperitif or to accompany a meal composed of light, fresh dishes. An ideal choice might be a tartar of white fish—bass or gilt-head—marinated in olive oil and lemon with a scattering of freshly grated ginger and sea salt. Simple yet sublime. The same joy can be had with crayfish in lemon butter with pickled fennel.

Through the simultaneously bold yet elegant shapes of its bottles and the delicate pastel shades of its wines, Ruinart has long viewed its champagnes as inspirational, quite apart from their intrinsic quality, even before the cork is popped. It therefore seems logical that the company has cultivated

FACING PAGE: *In the main courtyard of the headquarters on Rue des Crayères is a statue of Dom Thierry Ruinart, who inspired the founding of the firm, sculpted by Daphné du Barry (top).*
A portrait of company founder Nicolas Ruinart (1697–1769, bottom, left). It was Edmond Ruinart, representing the fourth generation of Ruinarts, who entered the American market in 1831 as witnessed here by the dedication to Roosevelt & Schuyler wine merchants, in New York (bottom, right).
PAGE 172: *The bottoms of bottles of Ruinart Blanc de Blancs, set on inclined racks while waiting to be "disgorged."*
PAGE 173: *The graphic precision of a dish devised by a chef at Lenôtre corresponds to the mineral elegance, finesse, and gustatory clarity of a vintage Blanc de Blancs.*

This EXQUISITE WINE of Champagne

A Drinking Song with Refrain

Composed by

Joseph Louis Mac Evoy.

Music Arranged by
S. J. ANDERSON.

Published by the Author

NEW-YORK.
K. DENHOFF.
44 WEST 29 ST.

BROOKLYN, N.Y.
GEO. A. KORNDER.
487 FULTON ST.

Chef Fabrice Brunet's Recipe

SEA URCHINS IN THEIR SHELLS, WITH SCALLOPS AND HERB AND SLOW-ROASTED TOMATO BUTTER

INGREDIENTS
Serves 4

- 4 sea urchins
- 2 scallops, shelled
- ⅛ oz. (4 g) arenka
- Olive oil
- 1 pinch (1 g) fleur de sel

Shellfish Salad:
- 4 razor clams
- 4 scallops, shelled
- Roe of 4 sea urchins
- ¾ teaspoon (3 g) shallots, stewed in butter
- 2 teaspoons (10 ml) white wine
- ½ teaspoon (2 g) finely chopped flat-leaf parsley
- Scant ½ cup (100 ml) scallop fumet

Scallop Stuffing:
- 2 oz. (55 g) shelled scallops
- ⅓ cup (90 ml) heavy cream
- ½ teaspoon (2 g) salt
- *Piment d'Espelette* or hot paprika

Herb and Slow-Roasted Tomato Butter:
- 1 stick (120 g) butter, well softened
- ¼ teaspoon (1 g) finely chopped garlic
- ½ teaspoon (1 g) finely chopped parsley
- ⅛ teaspoon (0.5 g) finely chopped tarragon
- ½ teaspoon (3 g) old-fashioned Meaux mustard
- 2 teaspoons (5 g) finely chopped slow-roasted tomatoes
- 1 teaspoon (3 g) finely chopped shallots
- Salt

METHOD
Carefully open the sea urchins and extract the roe. Clean the inside of the shells well and dry them.

Shellfish Salad: Place the shallots in a small saucepan with the white wine, the scallop fumet, and parsley and bring to a boil. Place the razor clams in the hot liquid briefly to open them then remove and set aside. Next poach the scallops over low heat, without allowing the liquid to boil, for 2 minutes.

Remove the scallops, slice them into four and place them in a mixing bowl. Cut the razor clams into angled slices and add them to the scallops with the sea urchin roe. Strain the cooking liquid through a chinois into a small saucepan.

Herb and Slow-Roasted Tomato Butter: Combine all the ingredients well. Chill for 30 minutes. Heat the cooking liquid from the salad and gradually stir it in.

Scallop Stuffing: Make sure that the bowl of the food processor is very cold. Process the scallops with the salt and *piment d'Espelette*. Pour in the cream in two additions.

To Finish: Add the butter with the cooking liquid to the shellfish salad. Half fill the cleaned sea urchin shells with the mixture. Using a pastry bag, pipe the scallop stuffing into the shells, shaping it into a dome.

Place in a dish half-filled with hot water and cover with plastic wrap. Cook at 250°F (120°C) for 20 minutes. While this is cooking, cut the remaining scallops into halves and marinade them in olive oil with fleur de sel. Top the filled shells with a half scallop and garnish with the arenka.

Note: Arenka is a transformed herring product that can be used as a substitute for caviar.

a close relationship with the arts ever since 1895, the year it commissioned a poster from Mucha. Having become the official champagne of numerous art fairs such as ARCO, Art Basel, and Art Basel Miami Beach, today it is highly present on the contemporary art scene under the leadership of its current president, Frédéric Dufour. This prestigious sponsorship is backed by a true commitment to the creative impulse, as witnessed by the many commissions for work from artists—painters, sculptors, photographers—during a special event or celebration. Thus the launch of the 2006 Prestige Collection set, composed of three champagnes ("R" de Ruinart, Ruinart Blanc de Blancs, and Ruinart Rosé), was accompanied by a "champagne spoon" designed by the talented India Mahdavi as a modern interpretation of the legendary silver spoon that, when placed in the open neck of the bottle, prevented the bubbles from disappearing. The following year, the great designer Christian Biecher came up with a bottle stopper that evoked the chardonnay flower, offered with a magnum of Ruinart Blanc de Blancs in a new version of the Prestige Collection set.

In 2008, Maarten Baas paid an amazing tribute to Dom Ruinart by devising a highly baroque version of an eighteenth-century centerpiece for a table: his crystal chandelier has fallen on the table amid candlesticks, champagne bottles, and coupes artfully arranged to defy the law of physics, logic, and conventional taste. The success of Baas' centerpiece inspired Ruinart to call upon the artist's skill the following year, to celebrate the fiftieth anniversary of Dom Ruinart. Baas came up with two leaning flutes that evoked the extravagance of his previous work yet could be included with Dom Ruinart 1998 in a special presentation case.

They were joined by another artwork produced in only fifty copies, namely "Melting Bucket," a centerpiece whose central element is a tilting, scintillating champagne bucket whose base seems to have melted on the tablecloth.

Ruinart expanded its initiatives in the field of art in 2010, the year that the Blanc de Blancs in the Prestige presentation case was adorned with an elegant "Gold Wire" design invented by the famous Patricia Urquiola. Inspired by the traditional wire retaining the cork she created a gilded cork snared in twisted gold wire that curves down the entire neck of the bottle. That same year, Nacho Carbonnel presented three works from his *Diversity* series at the VIP salon of the Art Basel Miami Beach fair. These variations on a piece of furniture that combines table and chair illustrated, through their spirit and materials, the Ruinart world: a sculpture of white paper evoking the purity of Chardonnay, another of rusty metal suggesting soil and vinestocks, and a third, created for Ruinart, composed of broken glass from Ruinart bottles. Ruinart has decided to be even more liberal in the freedom it grants to artists in their interpretation of the image of the oldest champagne house—it invites one or two artists every year to express, unfettered, their idea of what Ruinart means to them, via a sculpture, painting, or photograph. The resulting collection of artworks conveys in countless ways—yet with always the same intensity and creativity—Ruinart's quest for the absolute.

Chef Fabrice Brunet paired salty strips of sea urchins with the stony intensity of Dom Ruinart 2002.

PAGE 175: *The delicate flesh and creamy texture of shellfish heightened by the hint of a natural iodine flavor in this sea-urchin recipe was specially designed by chef Fabrice Brunet to match the slightly acid freshness, intensity, and length in mouth of a vintage Dom Ruinart 2002.*
FACING PAGE: *Thanks to a gastronomic partnership with Ruinart, Fabrice Brunet—the chef of the culinary lab at the famous caterer Lenôtre and winner of a national award for his work in 2010—invents and develops dishes designed to reveal the infinite aromatic finesse of Chardonnay champagnes.*

Cognac

HENNESSY

The pure white façade of this graceful, early nineteenth-century residence, surrounded by greenery, has a long, slim-columned verandah—you'd swear you were in Louisiana. Can the château de Bagnolet really be located in the Charente region of France, just a few miles from Cognac? Some startled visitors probably have difficulty believing it, especially on evenings when they hear strains of jazz or blues wafting on the breeze, or when they learn that Dee Dee Bridgewater, Willy Deville, or Mel Brown is holding forth in the grand salon. The locals, however, are in no way surprised by this "American touch." Distant voyages and exotic landscapes have always been part of the soul of cognac; the glamorous brandy has been circling the globe for centuries, tickling the most varied taste buds. Thus the château de Bagnolet, purchased in 1840 by Auguste Hennessy, grandson of the founder of the firm of that name, is a perfect symbol of the spirit of a vineyard, a town, and a region which are resolutely open to the world. As is the house of Hennessy itself, founded in Cognac in 1765 by Richard Hennessy, younger son of Charles Hennessy, lord of Ballmacmoy in Cork County, Ireland. Born in 1724, Richard served in the Irish brigade in France, composed of exiled Jacobites. On leaving the army at the age of thirty-two he returned to his family in Ostende in Flanders, a neutral port where trade was prospering, notably in the distribution of French and Spanish brandies destined for markets in England and Ireland. That is the business Richard carried out for nine years. Then, in 1765, he decided to trade in the most famous kind of brandy, made in Cognac, where he moved and set up a new operation.

Right from his first year of business, Richard Hennessy benefited from his family network: most of his brandies were shipped to London, Dublin, and Flanders. From that point onward the sole goal of the Hennessy firm has been to sell the best possible cognac to the widest possible market. During the 1770s a demand for truly grand brandies from Cognac arose, both in France and England. Such cognacs were not only aged but artfully blended, although the assemblage was still relatively simple. Hennessy was at the forefront of this development, according to records in the company archives that note a special consignment of brandy sent to Rochefort in 1777: this cognac was blended with a half-cask that had been aged for four years, "which improved the taste."

LONDON

October 14th 1817

SF

HRH
PR

Please note carefully the
following order to be shipped
to Mr Frederick Shore
of London for the account of
His Royal Highness
the Prince Regent
One puncheon of your
Very Superior Old Pale
Cognac eau de vie

F Shore

Two years later, a twelve-year-old cognac was delivered to a client in Paris. At the French court, the aristocracy began to discover the pleasures of fine old cognac by imitating the prince de Soubise, a great connoisseur. And then in 1787 Hennessy received his first order for a shipment to the United States.

Richard Hennessy's son, James, entered the business in 1784 at the age of nineteen, after a brief apprenticeship in Ostende. Four years later he was running the firm. With a new Irish partner, Samuel Turner, James would considerably expand the business over the following half century. When the French Revolution broke out, James expressed his sympathy for the cause—whether through conviction or a shrewd sense of business—and was a member of the National Guard delegation from Cognac that attended the famous Federation celebrations in Paris on July 14, 1790. Even after war broke out, he was able to sell his products on European and American markets, thereby insuring the profitability of his business. That was why, for example, he exploited the neutrality of the German port of Hamburg to shift his goods from Cognac to England, whence French products were re-distributed to northern Germany and the United States of America. Sales in North America have never flagged since that day.

Hennessy was determined not only to increase sales of cognac, but also to enhance its quality, encouraging the emergence of the concept of vineyard classifications, which would only become officially regulated by law in the early twentieth century. Several zones of production of cognac were distinguished, then ranked in a qualitative hierarchy. First come Grande Champagne and Petite Champagne, where vineyards that yield the best spirits are found; blends of these spirits are labeled "Fine Champagne." Then, in order of quality, come the vineyards of Borderies (to the north and west of Cognac), Fins Bois (encircling the three preceding zones), Bons Bois (an outer ring), and finally Bois Ordinaires (the coastal region). By the late 1780s, it was not unusual for Hennessy

Right from his first year of business, Richard Hennessy benefited from his family network: most of his brandies were shipped to London, Dublin, and Flanders.

clients to specify not only the age of the cognac but also its provenance—in 1789 the house of Timson & Tuffin in London ordered one hundred and fifty tierces of "champaign old best brandy."

On March 4, 1795, James Hennessy married Marthe Henriette Martell, daughter of Frédéric Gabriel Martell, the most powerful brandy merchant in Cognac. It was a marriage of love, overcoming the obstacle of religion—the Martells, originally from Jersey, were Protestants. The two families would always remain friends, often allies, and sometimes business partners. At the time of his marriage, James was already a rich landowner in Cognac and the surrounding area. Among other properties, in 1791 he bought part of a Franciscan monastery, including three small houses and the entire left wing of the main building, which would become company headquarters. The year following his wedding, he made his most important acquisition, an estate known as La Billarderie, located in Borderies, with a vast early eighteenth-century residence, extensive grounds, and vineyards, which still belong to the Hennessy family.

In 1813, James ended his partnership with Turner and founded a new company, Jas Hennessy, whose name would stick. Despite the Napoleonic wars that raged during this period, the English market remained by far the most important to Hennessy, accounting for over two-thirds of deliveries. Following the continental blockade of France and the fall of Napoleon's empire, with their understandably negative effects on business, Hennessy enjoyed a spectacular upsurge with the restoration of the monarchy. He acquired a solid

FACING PAGE: *In 1817, an enlightened connoisseur—namely the future King George IV of England—ordered some of Hennessy's "very superior old pale" cognac, which was the origin of the V.S.O.P quality label (top, left). The main entrance to the château de Bagnolet, built in the early nineteenth century. The warm, coppery colors of the hallway offer a fleeting reflection of the sparkle of cognac (top, right, and bottom).*

reputation and henceforth sold only top-quality cognacs. His list of glamorous clients included King George IV of England (from 1818 onward), the Russian imperial court in Saint Petersburg (from 1819 onward), and the duke of Norfolk (starting in 1825). In 1832, the prince de Talleyrand, then French ambassador to London, ordered "a case of thirty-six bottles of very old brandy." Historian André Castelot recounts an anecdote that is revealing not only of the famous diplomat's taste for cognac but also of the veneration already being accorded to distinguished brandies: one evening, one of Talleyrand's guests downed his glass of Fine Champagne in one swallow.

"That's not the way to drink cognac," said the prince. "You should take your glass in the palm of your hand, warm it, and swirl it around with a circular movement so that the liqueur releases all its aromas. Then you bring the glass to your nose—and inhale. And then...."

"And then, sir?"

"And then, sir, you set the glass down and discuss it...."

James Hennessy was henceforth not just a powerful merchant but also an important local figure, having enjoyed a brilliant political career between 1824 and 1842, when he was elected six times as the Charente representative to the national assembly. He died in 1843, and was followed in 1845 by his eldest son, James junior, whose health was weak. But James junior left three young children, including Maurice, who joined the family firm in 1853 at the age of eighteen, and who would be running it on his own by the 1870s. In the meantime, James senior's other sons, Auguste and Frédéric, piloted the business with notable rigor and dynamism. In 1833 Auguste had married Irène d'Anthès, daughter of a major landowner and aristocrat from Burgundy; it was Irène who inspired her husband to buy the handsome, exotic château de Bagnolet, in 1840. Auguste, like his father, was elected to the national assembly as the representative from Charente in 1848, after the

abdication of Louis-Philippe. As for Frédéric, in 1842 he married Julia Perkins, daughter of a major London merchant. Later, their daughter Marthe would marry Auguste's eldest son, Richard, thereby reinforcing family links. Furthermore, the first child from that union, Alice, born in 1873, ended up marrying Maurice's eldest son, James.

First come Grande Champagne and Petite Champagne, where vineyards that yield the best spirits are found; blends of these spirits are labeled "Fine Champagne."

The Second Empire in France was another boom period for Hennessy. The free-trade treaty signed between France and England in 1860 at Napoleon III's urging gave a considerable boost to English demand by lowering duties on brandy. Company sales in 1874 represented a quarter of all cognac exports, placing Hennessy in the number one position, way ahead of Martell. Cognac was now generally exported in bottles decorated with an "armored arm" (a feature from the family's coat of arms); labels were officially introduced in 1856. In order to respond to demand, the land devoted to winegrowing in Charente expanded significantly, reaching a peak of over 692,000 acres in 1877. It then represented France's most extensive vineyard. Unfortunately, in 1872 an aphid arrived from America, reached the vineyards of Charente, and by the 1880s it was wreaking considerable damage: the resulting phylloxera epidemic destroyed over 80 percent of the vine plants. Production of wine and cognac collapsed. Hennessy could only carry on trade by selling stocks of old cognac and buying up reserves available among winegrowers and distillers.

Maurice Hennessy, now head of one of the most powerful cognac firms, was on the front lines of the battle against phylloxera. He contributed

PAGE 184: *"The pavilion" next to the château de Bagnolet (seen through the stained-glass windows) features the traditional Hennessy coat of arms, the company founder. The famous "armored arm with broad ax" can just be made out above the crest.*
PAGE 185: *In the nineteenth century Hennessy was already the leading cognac firm in Europe, the United States, and Asia. In order to authenticate its bottles and protect its reputation, in 1856 the company began using labels bearing the name Ja^s Hennessy & Co. along with the "armored arm," which could be considered the company's first logo—and which still graces Hennessy labels today.*
FACING PAGE: *Next to the Renaissance-revival château de Bagnolet is another Hennessy family residence, now called "the pavilion."*

generous financial support to the research for remedies and was among the first people to advocate the radical solution of grafting French vines onto American rootstocks (those roots being resistant to the native phylloxera aphid). Several estates belonging to Hennessy, including La Billarderie, were placed at the disposal of researchers so that they could experiment with different varieties. There they carried out early tests with the Ugni Blanc grape, which was finally chosen for its good adaptation to the soil and climate. Maurice was soon joined in the battle by his eldest son James, born in 1867. In 1898 James became president of the winegrower's commission in the Cognac region, charged with encouraging local grape growers to replant by supplying them with free or inexpensive rootstocks. Little by little, the vineyards of Charente were reconstituted.

At the dawn of the twentieth century, one of the upshots of the phylloxera crisis was Hennessy's specialization in the manufacture and sale of cognacs that were several years old, the rich product of a series of subtle blendings—luxury cognac, in other words. Back in 1865, Maurice Hennessy had hit upon the idea of categorizing the names of his various cognacs while contemplating the fine window handles in his office, which were adorned with a star: one star henceforth indicated cognacs that were bottled after two years of aging, two stars indicated four years of aging, and three stars meant that the cognac had aged for six years prior to bottling. For cognacs older than six years, the company had already adopted what have become traditional names: V.O.P (very old pale), V.S.O.P (very superior old pale), and X.O (extra old). Over time, and through legal regulations, certain adjustments were made. Three stars became the equivalent of V.S, while V.O (very old) and V.S.O.P would require at least four years of ageing, and X.O at least six years. At Hennessy, these legal minimums are largely exceeded.

It was during this era that Hennessy combined its concern for quality with dynamic commercial policies. It prospected distant markets and by 1910

At the dawn of the twentieth century, one of the upshots of the phylloxera crisis was Hennessy's specialization in the manufacture and sale of cognacs that were several years old, the rich product of a series of subtle blendings—luxury cognac, in other words.

began to launch major advertising campaigns. The firm's marketing department was assigned to Jean Hennessy, Maurice's younger son, born in 1874, who steadily expanded the department and allocated it increasingly larger budgets. Hennessy Cognac was soon being sold on every continent: Australia became one of the firm's best outlets, while agents tirelessly covered Latin America and Africa. The doors to Asia began to open via India and Hong Kong, while China received its first barrels in 1859 and its first shipment of X.O in 1872. In the 1920s some prospecting was done in Japan, whose first order dated back to 1868, but the country only came to represent a significant market after World War II; for a few years prior to the economic crisis of 1990, Japan was even Hennessy's largest importer. In the United States, sales rose steadily until just after World War I, when prohibition put a serious brake on them. However, thanks to a new agent in New York, the Schieffelin company, which specialized in the sale of medication, Hennessy shrewdly skirted prohibition laws by selling a special cognac "for medicinal purposes." Following the great depression of the 1930s and World War II, the market in the U.S. began growing again and slowly outstripped sales in England.

Family tradition was respected by James and Jean Hennessy, both of whom led brilliant political careers alongside their business activities.

FACING PAGE: *Stretching away from the château is an extensive landscape garden that runs along the banks of the Charente River (top).*
Auguste Hennessy's beautiful, romantic wife, Irène d'Anthès (bottom, left), fell under the charm of the château de Bagnolet, where the couple moved in 1840 with their children. A nineteenth-century alcoholometric guide is still used as a reference source today (bottom, right).

STORED IN THE SHADOWS, DEMI-JOHNS
HOLD COGNACS OVER ONE HUNDRED
YEARS OLD THAT WILL BE BLENDED
WITH OTHER EAUX-DE-VIE TO CREATE
THE MYTHIC COGNAC CALLED RICHARD
HENNESSY.

ABOVE: *Making casks in the cooper's workshop (left). At the company headquarters in Cognac, a few brandies ready for tasting and grading by the master blender (right).*
FACING PAGE: *Demi-johns in the silence of the Founder's Cellar (built in 1771), where aged brandies wait patiently—some of them dating back to the 19th century—to be blended with others to create exclusive cognacs such as Richard Hennessy and Hennessy Paradis.*

James was elected to the national legislature as the representative for Charente, as was Jean in 1910. An enthusiastic internationalist and defender of the League of Nations, Jean was appointed French ambassador to Switzerland in 1924. Four years later, he was named minister of agriculture under French President Henri Poincaré. Meanwhile, James's son Maurice, born in 1896, studied in England before joining the company. Maurice ultimately became co-director with Jean, and played a key role in safeguarding stocks during World War II, laying the groundwork for the firm's extraordinary international growth in the post-war period. He also founded the Bureau National Interprofessionnel du Cognac (BNIC). In the 1960s, when the threshold of the sale of one million cases was surpassed, the reins were handed over to Jean's two sons, Patrick and Kilian (the latter becoming chairman of the board of Jas Hennessy at the end of that decade), alongside two of Maurice's nephews. Even today, Maurice's grandson Maurice Richard Hennessy is the firm's international ambassador while Kilian's son, Gilles Hennessy, is vice-president of Moët Hennessy, the group headed by Christophe Navarre.

Given post-war economic developments, these younger Hennessy generations realized that a corporation of this size was very difficult to manage, and even more difficult to pass on, as an exclusively family affair. An alliance was struck in 1971 with champagne producer Moët & Chandon, giving birth to the Moët Hennessy corporation, to be headed by a board of directors that included representatives of both firms. This period saw marked growth for Hennessy. In 1987, threatened by stock-market speculators, Moët Hennessy struck a deal with luxury leather-goods firm Louis Vuitton, which already owned the Spanish house Loewe and champagne-maker Veuve Clicquot, to form the LVMH group. Under the leadership of Bernard Arnault, LVMH would soon become the world's premiere luxury-goods corporation.

Summoned to take over the reins at Hennessy in 1997, Christophe Navarre imparted a new thrust to the company, allowing it to reassert its position of leadership far ahead of its rivals by innovating and developing new ways of drinking cognac in the United States and Asia. In 2001 Navarre was named president of Moët Hennessy, while the Hennessy branch is now run by Bernard Peillon.

The Founder's Cellar, the most prestigious of Hennessy's forty-two cellars, houses only the most outstanding cognacs that have already spent at least forty years in a standard cellar. There they will age yet longer, sometimes up to a century.

Just before the grape harvest, strolling among the vineyards of the La Bataille estate in the Grande Champagne district of Charente, one can idly imagine that the elixir made from these magnificent bunches of Ugni Blanc grapes will not be drunk until blended in a very old cognac—in a century or two. There are very few vineyards in the world where such a scenario is plausible. But here, on the 250 acres belonging to Hennessy, everything is done to make a very long life possible. It is said that 80 percent of the qualities, or defects, of a brandy are traceable to the quality, or defects, of the wine from which it is distilled. Hennessy's research department developed a model vinification unit in the 1990s with the goal of further improving the quality of the wine. Cognac is thus a wine that offers a glimpse of a distant future along with traces of the past, since it is the only one in the world produced as in days of yore, without the addition of antiseptics, which are incompatible

FACING PAGE: *The Founder's Cellar is where outstanding brandies that merit further ageing—sometimes up to one hundred years or more—are allowed to reside, as are the* coupe première *brandies that are still in the initial stage of assemblage (top). Cognac is the product of an assemblage, that is to say an artful blend of brandies of various estates and ages, made according to a* patron de coupe—*or reference sample—of the secret composition. The master blender is the architect of the assemblage, and Yann Fillioux today represents the seventh generation of Hennessy's master blenders (bottom, left). Every morning at 11:30 a.m. he convenes the tasting committee at Hennessy headquarters in Cognac; among the committee's noble tasks is the selection of new brandies submitted by suppliers called "deliverers" (bottom, right).*

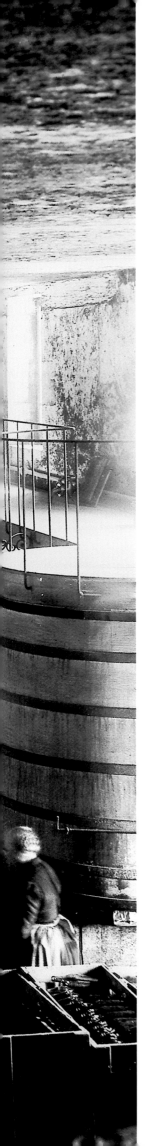

with an eau-de-vie of great quality. This criterion requires sufficiently acidic musts (acid being a natural antiseptic), impeccable hygiene throughout the entire vinification process, and great rapidity. Everything is designed to supply the distiller with an almost ideal wine, from gentle pneumatic presses to various decanting and fermentation vats. Hennessy's team of oenologists pay regular visits to the local winegrowers and distillers who traditionally supply the firm—known as "deliverers" of eau-de-vie—in order to explain the recommendations to be followed, since each year produces different grapes that require special vinification. Hennessy takes care to cultivate these winegrowers with their age-old traditions. Many of them supply Hennessy with new brandies—one famous supplier was the poet Alfred de Vigny who, in the mid-nineteenth century, sold to Hennessy the brandies produced on his estate of Maine-Giraud near Blanzac, where he is thought to have written his celebrated poem, "*La Mort du Loup*" ("Death of the Wolf").

Good cognac has always been conducive to journeying back in time. For starters, there is nothing like a visit to the Faïencerie cellars in Cognac, founded in the mid nineteenth century by Hennessy but named after an old faïence factory on the spot. A boat leaves from Hennessy's new quay-side building, which is a contemporary ode to cognac designed by Jean-Michel Wilmotte on the banks of the Charente. This handsome building is where the company receives visitors and displays various mementos of its history; it also hosts temporary exhibitions of works by great artists of the past and present, such as Savignac, Sempé, Poliakoff, Picasso, and Marc Riboud. A boat moored the foot of the headquarters makes it possible to cross the river to the cellars, notably the one called the Founder's Cellar. It is the most prestigious of Hennessy's forty-two cellars, and houses only the most outstanding cognacs that have already spent at least forty years in a standard cellar. There they will age yet longer, sometimes up

to a century. Sheltered by thick walls that shut out variations in temperature as well as noise, the air of the semi-dark cavern is thick with aromas. Visitors slowly file down long rows of casks bearing wonderful calligraphic marks in chalk that indicate the provenance of the cognac and its date of birth. Between the most recent—1953—and the oldest—1900—one takes the time to measure the patience and passion of makers of cognac who devote an entire lifetime to nurturing elixirs whose full maturity they will never know. Still further along are some demi-johns, lurking in the shadows. They hold cognacs that are over one hundred years old, which means that they are too old to continue to age in the wood of a cask; these venerable liqueurs—some of them dating back to the early nineteenth century—will no longer evolve, and therefore patiently await their fate in glass. Their fate, in fact, is rebirth, for they will be blended with other eaux-de-vie to create the mythic cognac called Richard Hennessy. An important part of the ingredients in this nectar date back to the nineteenth century: they are blended with art and science, bedded down in a cask for a further five years, and then made available in bottles to select connoisseurs around the world.

The five years during which old eau-de-vies mix and mingle take place in the most private, best protected part of the Founder's Cellar. All cellars in Charente have a special chamber or "chapel" where the most precious cognacs are prepared. At Hennessy, this is where the firm's other rare cognac is born. Hennessy Paradis is a very subtle assemblage of over one hundred very old eaux-de-vie. Whereas "Richard Hennessy" is a nectar of the gods with unmatched aromatic complexity and intensity, "Hennessy Paradis" is a full, round cognac of great finesse, offering an infinite spectrum of exquisite notes with a hint of spice. Such exceptional cognacs owe their existence to the skill of the master blender. That experience is like a venerable cognac itself, being several centuries old, handed down from

FACING PAGE: *A bottling workshop at the dawn of the twentieth century. Hennessy became the leading exporter of cognac in 1865, the year that the company set up it own bottling workshop. Maurice Hennessy, the director, came up with the idea of ranking cognacs according to number of stars.*

generation to generation within a single family for nearly a quarter of a millennium. Yann Fillioux, who joined the firm in 1967 in his uncle's footsteps, now represents the seventh generation. Flanked by a team of oenologists and experts, he is responsible for creating all of Hennessy's cognacs.

THE ALCHEMY OF SOIL, CLIMATE AND VINE

Centuries of tradition, combined with the right geographic location, the right climate, and very special soil has enabled the Charente region to produce an outstanding liqueur. As early as the third century BCE, the Romans had shrewdly taken advantage of its mild maritime climate and chalky soil to plant vineyards there. Several centuries later, ravaged by the Hundred Years' War and by competition from vineyards closer to the French capital, vineyards in Charente lost their way. They only began to revive in the seventeenth century, when major markets for local wines from Aunis and Saintonge suddenly opened in northern Europe as recompense for the support the region had shown for French Protestants after the revocation of the Edict of Nantes. Enthusiasm was nevertheless soon dampened: the wine sold poorly, for not only was it subjected to heavy customs duties but it didn't travel very well. An old habit of "burning off" excess wine—that is to say, distilling it—therefore became widespread.

Through what miracle did this local brandy acquire a reputation that, in a matter of decades, surpassed all those made in other regions of France and Spain? The often dazzling light that warms the rolling landscape of Charente offers a partial explanation of this mystery. Furthermore, on the finest winegrowing properties, namely the vineyards of Grande and Petite Champagne that run south from Cognac to the town of Jonzac, the white,

chalky surface of the soil reflects the sun and heat in a way that helps the grapes to mature and enhances their aroma. The nature of the fine, calcareous soil also creates unique conditions for the development of certain varieties of grape. Finally, the overall geographic position of the vineyards, sixty miles south of the Loire River and not far from the ocean, produces a warm, humid climate which, as far as grape-growing is concerned, is the perfect complement to the predominantly chalky soil. Nowhere else in the world is there this same alchemy of soil, climate, and light, which is best suited to certain varieties of grape. Formerly Folle Blanche grapes predominated, today Ugni Blanc plots are more extensive; once distilled, both varieties are capable of performing magic.

After geographical and natural conditions, the second crucial factor in the alchemy that led to the rapid triumph of cognac was the copper alembic used to distill wines. It was in the seventeenth century, and precisely in Charente, that a perfect alembic was devised, making possible a double distillation, one of the great secrets of cognac: the wine in the boiler is kept at boiling point for roughly twelve hours, during which alcoholic vapors rise into the large, onion-shaped, upper chamber and then pass into an elegantly curved tube (called a "swan neck" in French), and are cooled in a coil condenser (or "worm") from which drips the brouillis (or "low wine") with an alcoholic content of 27 to 30 percent (54 to 60 proof). The product of this first distillation is then returned to the still for another twelve hours in order to produce the brandy. After this second distillation only the "heart" of the spirit will be aged in casks, for the distiller takes care to eliminate the first gallons of the batch, the "head," which is considered too high in alcohol content, and the last gallons, the "tail," which is too low in alcohol. The result is an average spirit of 70 percent alcohol (140 proof), which is cooled before being transferred to the casks while the "head" and "tail" are added to the next batch of wine to be distilled.

PAGES 196 & 197: *For two and half centuries the expert hands of men and women have been shaping Hennessy's age-old universe. Here the master cooper completes the making of an oak cask using traditional tools (some of them a hundred years old). The cask will soon play host to a brandy which "matures" as it soaks up the aromatic richness of the oak's tannins.*
FACING PAGE: *The cool stillness of the shaded pergola on the grounds of the château de Bagnolet.*

This double distillation method is mandatory to earn the "cognac" label, and has been practiced in the same manner for three centuries. Meanwhile, the luscious taste of the finished product also depends on another art that was also perfected in Charente at a very early date—namely the process of ageing the brandy in oak casks. This is third crucial factor in the success of cognac. Locals say that it was the taste of brandy from a few forgotten casks that made people discover, in the early seventeenth century, the extraordinary improvement brought to cognac by ageing and by oak. The pores of the wood, in fact, allow for an interaction between the brandy and oxygen that leads to an evaporation of alcohol at a rate of two to three percent per year—called the "angel's share," a sacred offering to the passing of time. At the same time, the oak contributes the aromatic richness of the cognac's tannins. Concentrated by age and enriched with tannins, the mature brandy offers eye, nose, and palate a wonderful range of sensations that explains the value placed on cognac.

Thus, in addition to climate and geography, two noble, traditional materials, copper and oak, have helped to make cognac the finest of brandies over the past three hundred years. To all these secrets passed down through the centuries may be added another that has been enhanced over time—the art of tasting. This art is crucial to three important stages: the selection of the eaux-de-vie from those offered by suppliers; ageing, which requires regular tasting to guide choices (whether to use new casks or old, a damp cellar or a dry one, one blend rather than another); and finally blending, when it must be wedded to other brandies with a view to the final product. After the grape harvest, Hennessy's tasting committee selects the new brandies; between May and September, qualitative, and quantitative, assessments are made of the thousands of brandies in storage; and throughout the year, the blending of the various cognacs in the Hennessy range requires constant monitoring. So the tasting committee is permanently on duty. The committee meets every

In the mid-nineteenth century, Alfred de Vigny sold to Hennessy the brandies produced on his estate of Maine-Giraud near Blanzac, where he is thought to have written his celebrated poem "La Mort du Loup" ("Death of the Wolf").

morning at 11.30 a.m. in a special room at Hennessy headquarters in Cognac, the same room used for over fifty years. This committee is to cognac what the reading committee at Gallimard publishers was to French literature in the twentieth century: the most glamorous, most demanding, and most dreaded of juries.

Blending, or assemblage, is a noble and most complex task. The goal is to produce a consistent cognac that customers will recognize by blending brandies that are never the same from one year to the next. Connoisseurs of X.O, for example, expect to find the same cognac behind the same label today as they did yesterday or ten years ago, or indeed will find in ten years' time. Assemblage is done through a series of "cuts," getting ever closer to a sample that has been preserved; several initial blends of brandy are left to age, then re-blended together in variable proportions. The crucial preliminary step is selecting specific new brandies for a given cognac, and maturing them accordingly, for a given length of time, in old or new oak, or in a given cellar. Clearly, such a complex art, which requires accurate intuition, great experience, and perfect judgment, cannot be practiced by just anyone. The members of the tasting committe say that at least ten years of experience are required to guarantee that no major mistake will be made. After ten years, minor errors are still possible, indeed inevitable, but they can usually be corrected

FACING PAGE: *The distillery of Le Peu, a Hennessy property, perpetuates ancestral skills unchanged since the seventeenth century (top). You cannot call a brandy "cognac" unless it undergoes the double distillation process. Throughout winter into spring, wine is transformed into "eau-de-vie," or brandy, in copper alembics. At headquarters in the city of Cognac, guests are awaited for an unforgettable tasting experience conducted by one of the house experts (bottom).*
PAGE 203: *In Hennessy's forty-two cellars it is a tradition to write handsomely, in chalk, the origin and date of the finest brandies on the oak cask. The youngest of these exceptional brandies are already fifty years old, while the eldest nearly go back two centuries.*

The crucial thing about our craft is selection.
Suppliers propose their eaux-de-vie, we taste them, select or reject
them, and grade them—that grade determines their future.
It's our core job. This profession requires a passion for everything
good, everything beautiful, while always seeking the exceptional.
Creating a blend as qualitative as Paradis Impérial is intensely
satisfying, for it is the expression of all the values, dreams,
and joys of Hennessy's tasting team. Rather than artists who create
in a flash, we're builders or architects who insure the consistency
of a style by assembling complementary elements into something
beautiful and lasting. The enthusiasm of the people who choose
this profession constantly amazes me.

———————

Yann Fillioux
MASTER BLENDER

Tasting notes

PARADIS IMPÉRIAL: Inspired by a cognac made specially for Tsar Alexander I in 1818,
in fulfillment of an order placed by the tsar's mother, Tsarina Maria Feodorovna.
ASSEMBLAGE: based on an unusually high number of eaux-de-vie, including some
of the most distinguished brandies of the nineteenth and twentieth centuries.
COLOR: shimmering, subtle amber.
First nose: a bouquet of early-summer blossoms, jasmine, and orange flower.
ATTACK IN MOUTH: delicate yet persistent, revealing the extreme elegance of Paradis Impérial.
Floral overtones give way to a smoky note and a hint of spices.
PERFECT COMBINATIONS: goes well with Beluga caviar, white-meat fowl (flavored with
Jarnac truffles), foie gras, and very slightly warmed, sweet desserts.

by collective decision-making and by referring to the wisdom of the master blender. The nose and palate of the master blender ultimately serve as the sovereign yardstick. Given his four decades of tasting, and an even older familiarity with cognac—his uncle Maurice introduced him to the different aromas of casks when he was barely ten years old—Yann Fillioux knows how to prevent the tasting committee from losing its way in the forest of subjective judgments. For while one eau-de-vie is never identical to the next, the absolute value of the grade attributed to it must never vary.

Hence, the most highly appreciated cognac in the world comes into being. Hennessy cognac can be enjoyed in countless ways, depending on temperament, climate, or mood. The same X.O, a classic blend created over a hundred years ago—and whose bottle was brilliantly redesigned with curves in 1947 by Gérald de Geoffre—will be sipped straight in France or Britain, after a meal, sometimes with a good cigar, whereas in the United States and Asia it will be drunk as an aperitif, on the rocks or with a splash of water. Whatever the recipe, this rich nectar will yield all its power. In fact, in recent decades Hennessy has been able to invent new settings and new tastes for cognac, transforming its age-old image. The traditional French view of cognac, for instance, is diametrically opposed to the way it is seen in America. In places like Miami, San Francisco, and New York, the fashionable urban night crowd enjoys Hennessey in clubs and bars before taking a spin on the dance floor to the beat of a favorite DJ. American bartenders outdo one another to devise new cognac cocktails with ingredients such as Angostura bitters, ginger and apple juice, coffee liqueur and a shot of Coke, or sweet champagne. Anything goes. This highly creative "cocktail culture" is slowly and steadily gaining ground in Europe. Thanks to tips from Hennessy's taster, bartenders on both sides of the Atlantic are coming up with dozens of new cocktails based on the four flavors that are particularly suited to Hennessy: lime, apple, ginger, and raspberry.

Hennessy cognacs inspire not only bartenders, but also chefs. With his perfect command of the infinite range of aromas within his cognacs, Yann Fillioux, the master blender, is able to advise chefs such as the renowned David Fransoret, head chef at the château de Bagnolet. In one of the château's two charmingly restored dining rooms, guests can savor dishes both spicy and mild, smoky and tart, savory and sweet, all the fruit of recipes or combinations inspired by the rich palette of various cognacs: an invigorating coq-au-vin, first marinated then flambéed in X.O; or a light slice of pike-perch accompanied by pickled onion and a sauce of shallots and mushrooms, which are first flambéed in Hennessy V.S.O.P; or a croustade of foie gras enlightened by a glass of Paradis, to name just a few ideas.

Bartenders on both sides of the Atlantic are coming up with dozens of new cocktails based on the four flavors that are particularly suited to Hennessy: lime, apple, ginger, and raspberry.

Chef Fransoret travels worldwide, and receives international guests at Hennessy's table. Every style of enjoying cognac, on all seven continents, is not only tolerated but encouraged here. The Asian and Russian—and, more recently, American—custom of drinking cognac with a meal has been carried here to the heights of refinement. The X.O is present in discreet ways from first course to dessert, but is always tempered according to the dish, playing on contrasts of temperature by adding ice or water. With a first course of fried monkfish with piperade and a sauce of lemongrass, the X.O will be lightened by large splashes of water and three ice cubes. In contrast, between the first and second courses, an

FACING PAGE: *A view of the château de Bagnolet from the rear garden (top). Like a roving ambassador, chef David Fransoret travels the globe in search of the world's culinary traditions (bottom, left). He is convinced that there is a way to successfully wed every type of gastronomy to the endless range of aromas evoked by Hennessy cognacs. Here a strong, generous yet refined Richard Hennessy cognac (bottom, right) can bring its aromas of delicate flowers, spices, walnuts, and candied fruit to savory dishes seasoned with the likes of saffron, cardamom seeds, poppy seeds, mustard, and berries.*

ROASTED HEN, GARDEN VEGETABLES, TRUFFLES, AND IVORY SAUCE WITH X.O COGNAC AND TRUFFLES

INGREDIENTS
Serves 6

· I fattened hen, about 4 ½ lb. (2 kg)
· I tablespoon duck fat
· 3 tablespoons (50 g) butter
· 2 tablespoons X.O cognac
· I tablespoon curry powder
· Salt, *piment d'Espelette* (or hot paprika), pink peppercorns and Szechuan pepper

Aromatic Garnish for the Broth:
· 2 onions
· 2 shallots
· I stick celery
· I bouquet garni
· I head garlic
· I carrot
· 2 tomatoes
· 2 chicken stock cubes
· I cup (250 ml) white wine

Garden Vegetables:
· 3 large carrots
· I long turnip
· I zucchini
· I leek
· I oz. (30 g) Jarnac truffles for garnish

Ivory Sauce with X.O Cognac and Truffles:
· I ¼ cups (300 ml) chicken broth
· Scant ½ cup (100 ml) heavy cream
· 3 tablespoons (50 g) butter
· 2 teaspoons (10 ml) X.O cognac
· I oz. (30 g) Jarnac truffles, finely diced (brunoise)

METHOD

First prepare the hen. Remove each thigh and cut into two pieces. Take off the drumsticks and leave them whole. Cut the remaining carcass into two, leaving the breasts on the bone. Sauté the pieces of thigh and drumsticks in the duck fat and let cool. Vacuum pack them with butter and cook in the steam oven at 154°F (68°C) for 3 hours. Marinate the breasts with the cognac, curry, *piment d'Espelette*, salt, and peppers for 5 hours in the refrigerator. Brown them in a little more duck fat and finish the cooking at 195°F (90°C) for 1 hour, depending on the thickness of the meat. Set aside in a warm place.

Broth: Dice the vegetables into a mirepoix. Place them in the pot with the carcass and add the remaining ingredients. Cover with cold water. Cook for 2 hours. Strain through a chinois and reduce if necessary until the desired flavor is reached. Set aside in a warm place.

Cook the vegetables: Shape the carrots, turnip, and zucchini into regular ovals. Boil them in the broth. Cut the leek into angled slices and steam them. Cool over ice and reheat in the broth. Cut three generous slices of truffle per person and keep them warm in the broth.

Ivory Sauce with X.O Cognac and Truffles: Take 1 ¼ cups (300 ml) of the chicken broth and stir in the cream. Reduce for 10 minutes. Just before plating, whip in the butter and stir in the cognac.

To Plate: Open the vacuum pack and pour the contents into the ivory sauce. Let infuse for 10 minutes over low heat. Fillet the breasts and cut them into six identical pieces. Drain all the vegetables and arrange them in deep dishes or soup plates. Place a piece of thigh or drumstick and one piece of breast on each plate.

Strain the ivory sauce through a chinois. Add the finely diced truffles. Pour the sauce over the pieces of hen and add the sliced truffles.

intermediate dish (dubbed *le coup du milieu*)—say, a two-pepper sorbet (Tasmanian and Szechuan pepper)—will be served with X.O straight up. The main course, say a fillet of John Dory with olives, will call for a cognac with ice. The same drink will thereby create totally different impressions in the mouth throughout the meal. In order to fully appreciate the aromatic scope of X.O and the way it resonates with a given dish, the chef recommends preparing the palate with a sip of cognac, then tasting the dish, then taking another drop of the precious nectar. The full range of Hennessy cognacs enables Fransoret to remain open to recipes the world over without losing his own roots. In other words, he is able to invent "fusion food" made with cognac, which is encountering worldwide success. The very venerable, very rich tradition of Asian gastronomy, when judiciously wed to French cuisine, has produced results that even Chinese gourmets now appreciate. A traditional Chinese soup, always served at the start of a meal, carries a surprising scent of Charente—just before it is served the chef adds a little soy-and-cognac mixture. Cognac, in particular X.O, goes wonderfully with spicy Asian dishes, especially with their traditional spices of ginger and lemongrass. For example, a dish that made a big hit in Taiwan when Fransoret recently prepared it for a few dozen special guests was spicy pork cheek with candied ginger: the pork was first marinated for twenty-four hours, then flambéed with cognac before being cooked with spices and ginger.

Lighter cognacs with their fresh, maritime notes, such as V.S and V.S.O.P, are better with dishes of milder flavor, or else smoked or grilled food. Paradis, meanwhile, is perfect with warm, sweet flavors while the Fine de Cognac is better with cold sweets. Indeed, there is no dish that cannot be enhanced by the right cognac. Another factor, long tested in the kitchen, makes it possible

Cognac, in particular X.O, goes wonderfully with spicy Asian dishes, especially with their traditional spices of ginger and lemongrass.

to achieve the perfect balance, the ideal point where cognac and food meet without one overpowering the other: the moment when cognac is added to the recipe. If added at the start of the cooking process, the alcohol will evaporate and leave just a light, fruity taste; if added at the end, it will retain all its body and power.

At a table in the château de Bagnolet on any given evening you might come across a singer who has come to town for the Blues Passions festival in Cognac, an author celebrating the James Hennessy critics' award, or an American musician telling his last concert. Hennessy has friends and admirers all across the globe, and receives them with warmth and magnificence in the home that Auguste Hennessy bought out of love for his wife, the beautiful Irène d'Anthès. She died at the age of only thirty-six, some seven years after the château was acquired. Inconsolable, Auguste long refused to live in the château. Today, on a fine summer evening, after having enjoyed the hospitality of impeccable French-style service, dinner guests can now leave the table—a few hints of Jarnac truffles or Aquitaine caviar still on the tongue—and wander into the grounds of the château with a glass of Paradis in hand, there where Irène once strolled. Beneath the oak, linden, and cedar trees, among the fragrant magnolias and roses, this is the perfect place to enjoy an exclusive cognac perfumed with sweet scents of cinnamon and cardamom, wrapped in hints of honey and fruit. The perfect place, in short, to experience the magic of Hennessy.

PAGE 207: *Inspired by the universal nature of Hennessy cognacs, the house chef has invented dishes that combine the flavors of traditional French cuisine with those of Asia, the Middle East, and Latin America. Thus the woody, spicy, and peppery notes of X.O are delicately married here with the subtle, musky scent of black Jarnac truffles. But its aromas blossom equally well with the traditional spices and seasonings of Chinese cuisine.*
FACING PAGE: *Throughout the year the château de Bagnolet receives guests from every culture across the globe. In the lavish privacy of the summer dining room overlooking the grounds, every manner of appreciating cognac—which varies from one continent to another—are respected at Hennessy's table, making this spot the site of a timeless art of fine living.*

CHÂTEAU CHEVAL BLANC

On November 16, 2010, connoisseurs of great wines from all over the world gathered in a well-known auction house in Geneva, Switzerland, to witness the bidding on a treasure. An expert in the famous auctioneer's wine department had described this gem as "without a doubt one of the greatest bordeaux of all time." By the time the hammer came down, a record had been set for the most expensive bottle of wine ever sold: a collector had just spent a little over 300,000 dollars! Obviously, the bottle—an imperial magnum, containing the equivalent of eight ordinary bottles—was a legendary vintage from a legendary vineyard, namely a 1947 Château Cheval Blanc. This wine from Saint-Émilion, with its extraordinary flavors of candied fruit, was powerful and spicy yet as soft as cashmere, and lasted forever in the mouth. Not only was this wine at its height, it could remain so for another hundred years.

The passions aroused by Cheval Blanc are matched by its unique personality and delectable complexity. Rated a *premier grand cru classé A* since 1955, the year Saint-Émilion wines were first ranked, this wine is intense in both nose and mouth and combines, like no other wine, strength and smoothness with freshness and length in mouth. It not only ages well, as do all great wines, it ages exceptionally well. What explains such peerless qualities? Why Cheval Blanc rather than another wine made from the vineyards that stretch for 13,000 acres around the fine medieval city of Saint-Émilion in the Bordeaux region of France?

In order to answer these questions, we have to flash back to an earlier stage in the life of our planet, or, more precisely, the beginning of Quaternary period roughly two million years ago. At that time rivers swelled, overflowed, and branched out, creating an almost delta-like landscape in what is now the Pomerol-Saint-Émilion region. The limestone plateau that now underlies most of the highly ranked growths was spared, while lower down a tributary of the Dordogne River known as L'Isle carried sediments from its source in the hilly Massif Central. These sediments were variously deposited, depending on local terrain—in the area immediately around Cheval Blanc, Figeac primarily caught pebbles whereas La Dominique largely received sand and Petrus to the north was steeped in clay. Meanwhile, what is today the Cheval Blanc property—an unbroken patch of eighty-eight acres of vineyard—is uniquely complex

A RECORD HAD BEEN SET FOR THE MOST
EXPENSIVE BOTTLE OF WINE EVER SOLD:
A COLLECTOR HAD JUST SPENT A LITTLE
OVER 300,000 DOLLARS!

ABOVE: *Detail of the orangery, one of the château's outbuildings, which dates from the nineteenth century (left).*
The entrance hall of the château (right).
FACING PAGE: *A detail of the original fresco in the Red Salon. The theme evokes the traditional name of the spot—Cheval Blanc*
("white horse")—where vineyards were planted in the eighteenth century, as inscribed on royal maps of the day.

in its diversity: a diagonal of green and blue clay cuts across it, but it also has pebble-strewn mounds and a sandy stretch above a clay subsoil. This complexity, spread across some fifty separate plots vinified individually, blossoms forth on tasting a wine that displays all the aromatic richness and smoothness of clayey soils as well as the tannic sophistication and length in mouth associated with stony soil.

This basic reason for the unique character of Château Cheval Blanc was brilliantly exploited in the latter half of the eighteenth century by a man of genius, Jean Laussac-Fourcaud. In 1852, this wine merchant from Libourne married Henriette Ducasse, daughter of the chief judge of the local court, who brought as her dowry some seventy-five acres of vineyard. Twenty years earlier, Judge Ducasse had purchased a forty-acre stretch of vineyard from Comtesse Félicitée de Carles-Trajet. The land was on a part of her Château Figeac estate known as Cheval Blanc. This vineyard represents the start of the saga of a great wine. Six years later, in 1838, Judge Ducasse bought an additional thirty-five acres. But he was very busy with his judicial activities and he left his vines in the care of Mother Nature and ancestral practices (a map drawn up in 1764 by the royal geographer, Pierre de Belleyme, shows that grapes were already being grown on this spot). The judge's new son-in-law, however, was a wine merchant who knew a thing or two about vines and land, and he decided to reinvigorate the overlooked vineyard that he now found in his possession. Laussac-Fourcaud began with a detailed observation of the diversity of his vineyard, noting the qualities of certain plots that needed to be enhanced, and the drawbacks of others that needed to be corrected. Among those drawbacks was too much water, which induced him to install a drainage system made of ceramic pipes, traces of which can still be found today. Laussac-Fourcaud's second brilliant idea was to replace the traditional Merlot grapes—the main variety in that

Rated a premier grand cru classé A since 1955, the year Saint-Émilion wines were first ranked, this wine is intense in both nose and mouth and combines, like no other wine, strength and smoothness with freshness and length in mouth.

area—by Cabernet Franc vines (here known as Bouchot). Perhaps this decision was inspired intuition, or perhaps sparked by fear of the vine deformation and gray rot that so often attacked the highly sensitive Merlot. Maybe it was simply a reasonable decision to plant his land with a grape that ripened later, thereby balancing the early ripening Merlot. Or maybe he simply wanted to give his wine an original touch. We don't know the exact reason. Whatever the case, Laussac-Fourcaud's decision to devote roughly sixty percent of his vineyard to Cabernet Franc while keeping the other forty percent in Merlot, completed in 1871, was a perfect response to the complexity of the soil. And it hasn't changed since, for very good reasons: when combined with the vineyard's geological diversity, this breakdown makes Cheval Blanc a unique Saint-Émilion and a singular sensory experience. The round, full, velvety qualities of Merlot are transported, then refined, by the freshness and finesse of Cabernet Franc grapes. At the same time, this particular mix of grape varieties adapts itself to the climate, making it possible to produce a wine that is not only one of the most consistent in the world but also of great quality whatever its age.

Along with his inspired vineyard work, Laussac-Fourcaud built an elegant house on the edge of his land. Relatively modest in size but

PAGES 216–217: *Behind the château can be seen the gentle curves of the estate's new white concrete winery, dubbed "the cellar beneath the hill" by its designer, architect Christian de Portzamparc. Completed in time for the 2011 harvest, it weds the geometry of the vineyards that encircle it in an unbroken mosaic of eighty-eight acres.*
FACING PAGE: *In addition to the legendary year of 1947, the estate has regularly produced exceptional vintages now highly prized by wine lovers throughout the world, such as 1959, 1982, 1989, and 1998.*

harmonious in proportions, and soon flanked by a chapel, Château Cheval Blanc was completed in 1860. The winemaker immediately gave the château's name to his wine, previously marketed as "wine of Figeac." It fully merited its new aristocratic name, having been worthy of neighboring châteaux for a number of years already. The appeal of the wine's outstanding qualities were already becoming known, and it would soon go on to win numerous medals, notably at the universal expositions held in London in 1862, Paris in 1878, and Antwerp in 1885.

When Jean Laussac-Fourcaud died in 1893, his son Albert succeeded him. For some unknown reason, the son reversed the family name, becoming Albert Fourcaud-Laussac. He followed in his father's footsteps and carried the château to the height of fame with great vintages such as 1899 and 1921. His wife Louise Chaperon, daughter of a successful wine merchant from Libourne, enabled Albert to buy out his seven brothers, thereby avoiding the breakup of the vineyard, which he transformed into a non-trading sharehold. He also installed twelve wooden vats, which would remain there until 1966. On Albert's death in 1926 his son Jacques became manager of the château while his younger brother Joseph was in charge of the vines and winemaking. Shortly afterward, in 1929, Cheval Blanc produced one of its historic vintages. From 1943 onward Joseph was assisted by cellar master Gaston Vaissiere; together, the two men made several legendary vintages, such as the famous 1947, described above as "one of the greatest bordeaux of all time."

Joseph's daughter, Claude Fourcaud-Laussac, gave an account of the almost miraculous birth of the vintage 1947 in a moving book, *Au Cheval Blanc—Une Histoire de Millésimes* (Cheval Blanc: A History of Vintages), published in 1998. "It was a miracle child. Everything happened like magic: fermentation, malolactics, the reduction of sugar despite the high temperature. And yet in that post-war period we lacked casks, among other

things.... Fortunately, the Merlots were extraordinarily fruity and the Cabernet Francs were of rare finesse." A few lines later, the author perhaps supplied one of the keys to the mystery. "I'll never forget the harvesting that year. It took place under a scorching sun, between September 15 and October 4. We were hot, and we were celebrating, with huge bursts of laughter that still ring in my ears. Everyone sensed that we were going to witness the birth of a great among greats." In fact, the grapes that year enjoyed exceptionally fine weather throughout the growth cycle from April to late October. The vinification would fully—astonishingly—benefit from the grapes' concentration and extreme sweetness.

The famous wine critic Robert M. Parker called the 1964 "the most authoritative Cheval Blanc of the 1960s and '70s."

As years went by, so did great vintages, in particular 1961 (one of the most accomplished) and 1964 (which famous wine critic Robert M. Parker called "the most authoritative Cheval Blanc" of the 1960s and '70s). The 1980s were notable for vintage 1982, which benefited from hot, dry weather right up to harvesting time, and thus presents a broad spectrum of contrasting taste impressions in which smoky, roasty, and spicy flavors do not impede a fresh, creamy, fruity wave that lasts forever on the palate.

In those years the estate belonged to some forty family shareholders, and was run by an emblematic figure in Bordeaux, Jacques Hébrard. Hébrard was an eminent member—indeed, the *premier jurat*—of the twelfth-century guild known as the Jurade de Saint-Émilion, which was the supreme authority over this appellation. Under his aegis, in 1988 the estate began producing a second wine, dubbed Petit Cheval.

FACING PAGE: *Interior views of the chapel next to the château (top, left, and bottom, right). The light, foliate curves of the new winery rising from ancestral lands establish a symbiosis with the ordered lines of the château erected a century and a half earlier (bottom, left, and top, right).*

Wine lovers soon sought it out for its obvious family resemblance to its older sibling. It "opens" more quickly, of course, yet also delivers the familiar complexity and finesse, fresh and round. Its high quality is due to the fact that it is no ordinary "second" wine—the batches of grapes that go into it are not chosen because they are inferior to the "great wine," but simply because they do not create an ideal synergy with those grapes already selected for the latter. The existence of a third wine, for that matter, is a guarantee of the quality of Petit Cheval. These second and third wines represent nearly half of the vineyard's total harvest.

When Hébrard retired in 1991, the family employed Pierre Lurton to replace him. Then aged thirty-four, the scion of a great family of winemakers, Lurton had just spent twelve years running a family estate, Clos Fourtet, whose wine was ranked as a Saint-Émilion *premier grand cru classé.* The next year Lurton hired the Dutch oenologist Kees van Leeuwen, a great specialist in Saint-Émilion wines, to be his technical director. The work they put in bore fruit in the hot, dry year of 1995, which produced a sublime Cheval Blanc, followed by outstanding vintages in 1998, 1999, and 2000.

Those three great years were the felicitous start of a new era at Cheval Blanc. In 1998, in fact, two old friends jointly purchased, in a private capacity, this crown jewel of Saint-Émilion vineyards. One was Bernard Arnault (whose shares would be bought by the LVMH group in 2010), the other was Baron Albert Frère. Both men—one the president of LVMH and the other a Belgian businessman with stakes in all the leading financial and industrial firms in Europe—were highly cultured and enamored of traditional skills, and they had long been seeking to acquire an exclusive vineyard. When the opportunity arose to buy Château Cheval Blanc from the Fourcaud-Laussac family, they jumped at it. The wine had reached such a height of excellence and fame that their first decision was to do absolutely nothing—apart from renovating the interior of the château, fully respecting its original style and soul, the better to receive distinguished guests. The management team, however, remained intact.

GROOMING A THOROUGHBRED

The Château Cheval Blanc team then undertook the highly demanding task of perpetuating the vineyard's genetic heritage while refining all its qualities. A vine stock at Cheval Blanc lives, on average, a little over forty years. The vineyard must therefore be replanted yet retain its own DNA, that is to say using its own plant stock. At Cheval Blanc the traditional home-cutting system, known as *sélection massale,* is employed, which generally means selecting the best vines and cutting shoots that are then replanted. A veritable library of Cabernet Franc stock has been built up from cuttings taken from very old vines, some almost a hundred years old—the oldest stocks date from 1920—yet still in production. The chosen plants must display ideal qualities: they must be modest in yield, producing smallish bunches with grapes that are well colored and harmoniously arrayed. A rigorous clonal selection process over a long period of observation, which includes making micro-batches of wine, finally leads to a slow but steady replanting of "optimized" vine shoots. Only two and a half acres are renewed every three years, in order not to disturb the quality and diversity of the vineyard, which are key to its identity. The high average age of the carefully preserved vines thus limits yield to less than forty hectoliters per hectare (roughly four hundred and fifty gallons per acre).

Here the crucial work takes place in the vineyard. Throughout the year a team of twenty

PAGES 222–223: *The curved tip of the new winery points to the orangery, chapel, and château. The vineyards can be glimpsed in the background, behind the garden.*
FACING PAGE: *Viewed from the grassy summit of the new winery, the vineyards stretch to the horizon.*

moves among the vines, whereas only three or four people are needed to monitor the winemaking in the cellar. A great wine is first and foremost the product of great grapes. Growing such grapes in a vineyard where weed killers have never been tolerated and insecticides are limited to a strict minimum calls for constant labor. Tasks are determined by two weather stations installed on the estate, providing highly precise data on a daily basis. In addition to the four seasonal plowings of the earth, work in a vineyard involves regular pruning, notably including a "de-budding" operation that eliminates one of every two buds, in order to spread out the bunches and reduce the risk of rot. Old wood is pruned twice a year, and in June the leaves are thinned on the east-facing side. In July, bunches that touch are spread out to avoid the formation of "packets" of grapes. A little later, as the day of full ripeness approaches, imperfect or late-developing bunches are removed.

The exact date of harvest is determined by preliminary sampling. Done exclusively by hand, picking will begin when the Merlot grapes are perfectly ripe, toward the end of summer or early autumn (the earliest date being September 1 in the "heat wave" year of 2003, the latest being October 13 in 1980). The Merlot harvest is followed by the Cabernet Franc, which ripens later. Whatever the case, the picking period is never the same from one year to the next, and even varies from one plot to the next depending on ripeness, which is established on a day-to-day basis that calls not only for an acute sense of observation but also great flexibility and speed on the part of the pickers. The estate's eighty-eight acres require ten to eleven actual days of picking, often spread over a period of three weeks or more. Harvesting is thus a process of continuous selection, only the chosen grapes going to the cellar on a given day. In Cheval Blanc's new cellar, opened in 2011, the grapes are first weighed then stored in a cold room. Once the entire plot has been picked, the

At Cheval Blanc, since the harvest of 2011, all these ancestral tasks have taken place in a cellar that is a vast work of modern art. It was designed and built by one of today's greatest architects, Christian de Portzamparc.

grapes are placed in a vat most suited to their weight (from a choice of nine different capacities).

Vatting—or fermentation on the skins—lasts approximately three weeks and entails a gentle, measured extraction of the grapes' color and tannins. The wine is tasted daily during this process of maceration in order to determine the exact moment when it will be run off into another vat for malolactic fermentation. Then, in November or early December the wine is transferred to casks where it remains for fifteen to eighteen months. Cheval Blanc uses only casks made of French oak, supplied by six different coopers. In January or February the wine is racked for the first of five times, which means it is clarified upon being transferred from one cask to another. At various times the casks also need topping up, which means replacing wine that has evaporated in order to forestall oxidation. As spring approaches, following numerous tastings by a team of specialists that includes outside consultants as well as château oenologists, the cellar master must get down to the crucial operation, namely the highly tricky blending, or assemblage, of wines from the different grapes and plots of the estate. He will endow the vintage with its complexity and specific personality. Before being bottled, the wine is racked a fifth time and then fined, which means adding

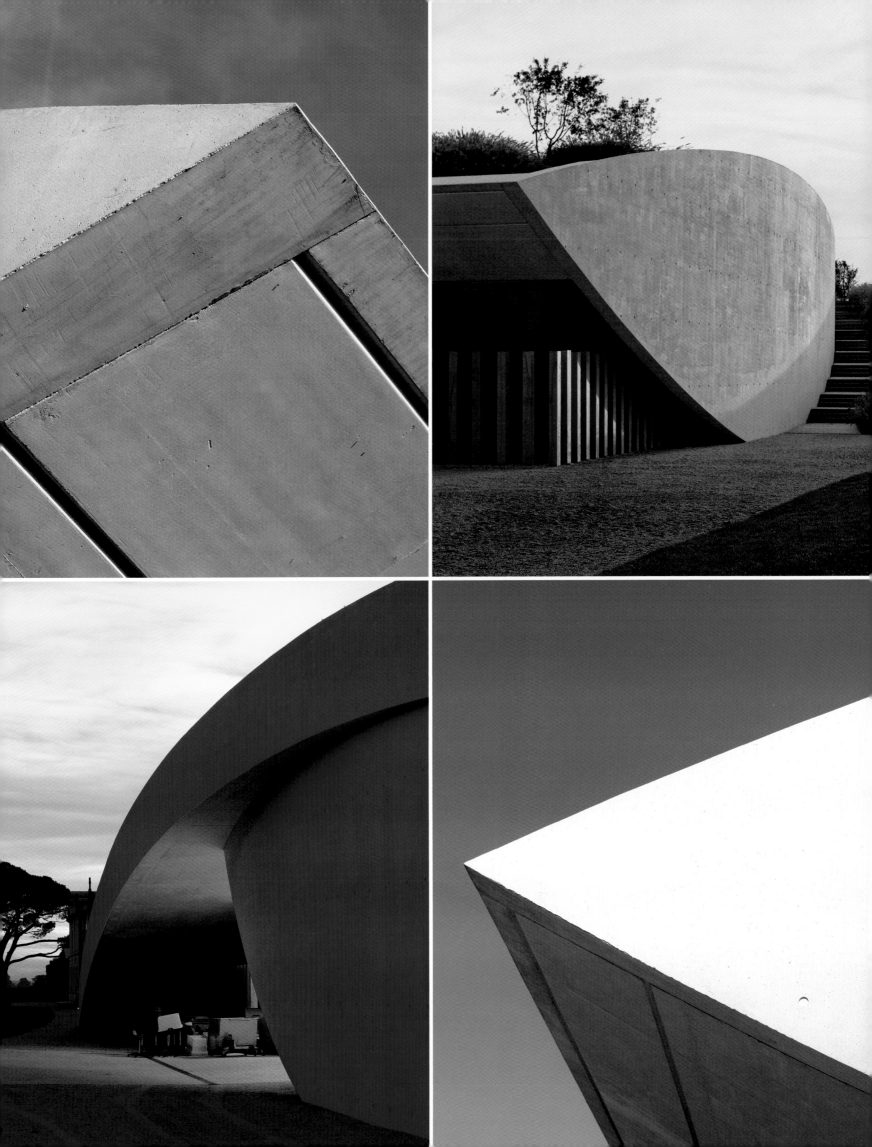

There has never been a break in the style
of Château Cheval Blanc since 1832. My job involves insuring
its qualities of freshness and elegance—what Pierre Lurton
liked to call its cashmere softness—and its aging potential.
It's all a question of fine tuning. The details are what
make the difference between a good wine
and a great wine. The raw materials are there, the soil and climate
are exceptional. But even good ingredients won't make a delicious
dish if you don't cook them the right way. The main thing
is to get the best out of each year—you have to pick each plot when
it is perfectly ripe. Managing degrees of ripeness is the sinews
of this particular war! Château Cheval Blanc is a wine for laying
down. If tasted young and compared to a wine only slightly
inferior, the difference won't be enormous.
But twenty-five years later, they're worlds apart.

––––––––––

Pierre-Olivier Clouet

CELLAR MASTER

Tasting notes

VINTAGE: 2009
HARVEST: *Dry, stable weather in September; fully ripe grapes on Cabernet and Merlot vines;*
highly selective picking based on day-to-day tastings.
FIRST NOSE: *Complex, notes of black fruit, spices, licorice, and mint.*
ATTACK IN MOUTH: *Full and powerful; extremely smooth tannins.*
PERFECT COMBINATIONS: *Noble fish such as sea bass, John Dory, and, turbot; game with*
a fricassee of mushrooms (girolles or morilles).

two or three beaten egg whites to the cask in order to draw any remaining particles to the bottom.

At Cheval Blanc all these ancestral tasks are done with the greatest respect for the noblest tradition of winemaking, yet since the harvest of 2011 they have taken place in a cellar that is a vast work of modern art. It was designed and built by one of today's greatest architects, Christian de Portzamparc. In line with the château, Portzamparc erected a gently sloping, grass-roofed mound whose silken-white concrete sides billow like sails, creating an oval symmetry that harmonizes perfectly with the horizontality of the surrounding vineyards. The apparently endless extent of those vineyards can be seen from the top of this "cellar beneath the hill," whose summit is easily reached. Inside the cellar itself, natural light illumines the spirit of the place, and visitors realize that the beauty of the building and the great care taken with every detail reflect an artistry entirely geared to the making of wine in a rational and functional way. Below ground, the open-work walls of the cask cellar facilitate natural aeration. In the vat room are fifty-two vats—with sensual curves that evoke concrete sculptures—ready to receive, at the exact moment of maturity, the steady flow of grapes from the estate's forty-four different plots. Highly demanding environmental criteria have been respected in terms of managing water, energy, and waste, as have considerations of the acoustic, visual, and olfactory comfort of the people working in the cellar. Cheval Blanc's new cellar is thus one of the few buildings of its kind to receive a certificate of "high environmental quality" (HQE).

Every year the château receives roughly five thousand guests for lunch or dinner—owners and their friends, clients and suppliers, wine journalists, celebrities, and so on. The chefs are charged with devising menus to accompany one or several vintages of Château Cheval Blanc without comprising the wine's aromatic palette and silken,

A vine stock at Cheval Blanc lives, on average, a little over forty years. The vineyard must therefore be replanted yet retain its own DNA, that is to say, using its own plant stock.

velvety texture. The chefs meet this challenge with great humbleness but also with great skill. Cheval Blanc regularly invites chefs to devise new menus, such as Jean-Baptiste Depons (also chef at Yquem) and Philippe Etchebest (chef at the Michelin two-star L'Hostellerie de Plaisance in Saint-Émilion, and winner of a *Meilleur Ouvrier de France* award). In fact, the power and freshness of the wine allows for almost every combination—including fish. The latter must however be chosen from among the noble varieties such as sea bass, monkfish, John Dory, and turbot, which can be roasted or cooked in meat juice. Game, red and white meat, and cheese are all obviously natural matches, mushrooms of various types (*girolles, morilles*) either raw or fricasseed (perhaps with game stock in the latter case). Depons notes that guests are always delighted by the perfect marriage of Cheval Blanc with truffles. Potato purée with truffles has become one of the château's classic dishes to accompany both fish (turbot or monkfish) and meat (prime cut of beef, filet mignon, or veal chop). A glass of Petit Cheval, almost always served with the first course, is also a perfect match with truffles, for example flavoring an egg soufflé whose creaminess enhances the silkiness of the wine. Although Cheval Blanc's personality probably makes it a wine more suited to fall and winter than summer, it can accompany with great subtlety red berries on a hot day. In winter, all desserts made of apple or pear are feasible, but chocolate is particularly good on the assumption that it is dark,

FACING PAGE: *The grassy roof of the new winery shelters sorting hall, vat house, and tasting room (top). All have been in full swing since September 2011 under the skilled leadership of Pierre Lurton (bottom, left). Harvests at Cheval Blanc are done exclusively by hand in a continual process of selection. Grapes are selectively picked on the plots, then are sorted again on arrival at the winery, first bunch by bunch then grape by grape (bottom, right).*
PAGES 232–233: *After the harvest, wine from various plots is stored in casks made exclusively of French oak for a period of fifteen to eighteen months, on the lower level of the new winery. The openwork walls favor natural aeration.*

AT CHEVAL BLANC A VERITABLE LIBRARY
OF CABERNET FRANC STOCK HAS BEEN
BUILT UP FROM CUTTINGS TAKEN
FROM VERY OLD VINES, SOME ALMOST
A HUNDRED YEARS OLD.

ABOVE AND FACING PAGE: *The vat house in the new winery. The fifty-two cast concrete vats receive grapes from the estate's forty-four plots progressively, at just the right moment of ripeness. The building is one of the few of its kind to have received a certificate of "high environmental quality" (HQE).*

slightly bitter and not too sweet (70 percent cocoa content is ideal). The chefs at Château Cheval Blanc thus regularly serve dark chocolate desserts in the form of creamy cakes, mousses, crepes, sherbets, and other delights, wed to carefully selected vintages from the wine cellar.

Chefs at Cheval Blanc favor French cuisine, which is what their guests most often wish to experience and which also seems at first sight to be the most suited to the local soil and climate as expressed in the wine. Great classic dishes, straightforward yet delicious, are often found on the menu, such as a prime cut of beef Rossini with eggplant caviar, roast baby pigeon with cumin-seasoned vegetables, slow-roasted shoulder of lamb, sea bass with zucchini carbonara, black pork belly with Périgueux sauce, rib roast of Bazas beef with half-cooked "Tête Noire" mimits, and so on. However, assuming that care is taken not to overwhelm the wine with extreme flavors, Château Cheval Blanc can be drunk with culinary dishes from all over the world. Pierre-Oliver Clouet, the château's technical director, and Arnaud de Laforcade, its financial and marketing director, have recently confirmed this observation—by default. During a trip to China, they tasted a traditional sweet black rice cake that included dates and raisins as well as red-bean paste, and they suddenly realized that something was missing: a glass of Cheval Blanc whose flavors of candied fruit and whose smoothness would have provided a perfect echo to this exotic treat.

Ken Hom, the grand chef of Chinese cuisine who loves both Yquem and Cheval Blanc, has realized that the marriage of his inventive dishes to the famous wine from Saint-Émilion can be a rewarding experience. He recommends it whenever feasible, notably with his version of Peking duck (a local specialty now found throughout China), whose rich flavors and textures are a perfect match for the complexity, finesse, and fruity freshness of Cheval Blanc. The duck fat is meticulously removed during cooking, so all that remains is the tender meat with its thin, crusty skin coated in a traditional sauce of lemon, honey, soy sauce, and rice wine. The duck is served with spring onions and wrapped in a thin pancake seasoned with sweet hoisin sauce, allowing this thoroughbred from Bordeaux to gallop gleefully across the Asian steppes.

Whatever the case, the picking period is never the same from one year to the next, and even varies from one plot to the next depending on ripeness, which is established on a day-to-day basis and calls for an acute sense of observation.

FACING PAGE: *The tasting room in the new winery is a nerve center where the fate of a vintage is determined (top). As spring approaches, the cellar master and his team of oenologists conduct the highly tricky assemblage, or blend, of the estate's various plots of two great varieties of grape, Merlot and Cabernet Franc. This operation will define that vintage's specific personality and complexity. Cellar master Pierre-Olivier Clouet (bottom, left). A tasting room within sight of the vineyards awaits Château Cheval Blanc's guests (bottom, right).*

RIB ROAST OF BAZAS BEEF WITH HALF-COOKED "TÊTE NOIRE" PORCINI

INGREDIENTS
Serves 6

· 3 ¼ lb. (1.5 kg) rib roast
· 2 lb. 10 oz. (1.5 kg) "tête noire" porcini (*Boletus aereus*)
· A little olive oil
· 1 ¾ lb. (800 g) veal trimmings
· A little peanut oil
· 2 sweet onions, chopped
· 4 tablespoons (60 g) unsalted butter
· 3 cups (750 ml) red wine
· 3 oz. (80 g) gray shallots, chopped
· A few sprigs chives, chopped
· Salt and pepper

METHOD
With a clean, damp cloth, carefully clean the porcini. Set aside the three most attractive for decoration. Cut the remaining porcini into slices just under ½ inch (1 cm) thick. Heat a little olive oil. Quickly sear the sliced porcini in the olive oil and transfer them to a colander. *Make a* jus: Cut the veal trimmings into large pieces. Sear them in a little peanut oil over high heat. Add the chopped onions and butter. Deglaze with the red wine and add water to cover. Simmer over low heat for about 1 hour 30 minutes. Strain the liquid and reduce it. Adjust the seasoning and set aside in a warm place. Preheat the oven to 350°F (180°C).
Heat a little olive oil in an ovenproof pot until it is smoking. Brown the joint of beef. Cut the three reserved porcini in half lengthwise and add them to the pan. Place the rib roast and porcini in the oven for 6 to 7 minutes to finish cooking, depending on the thickness. Reheat the cooked porcini with a little butter and the chopped shallots. Season with salt and pepper. When the porcini are hot, sprinkle with the chopped chives. Carve the beef into slices. Arrange a pile of sliced porcini at the bottom of each plate. Place the rib roast over and top with a half porcini. Drizzle with reduced *jus* and serve immediately.

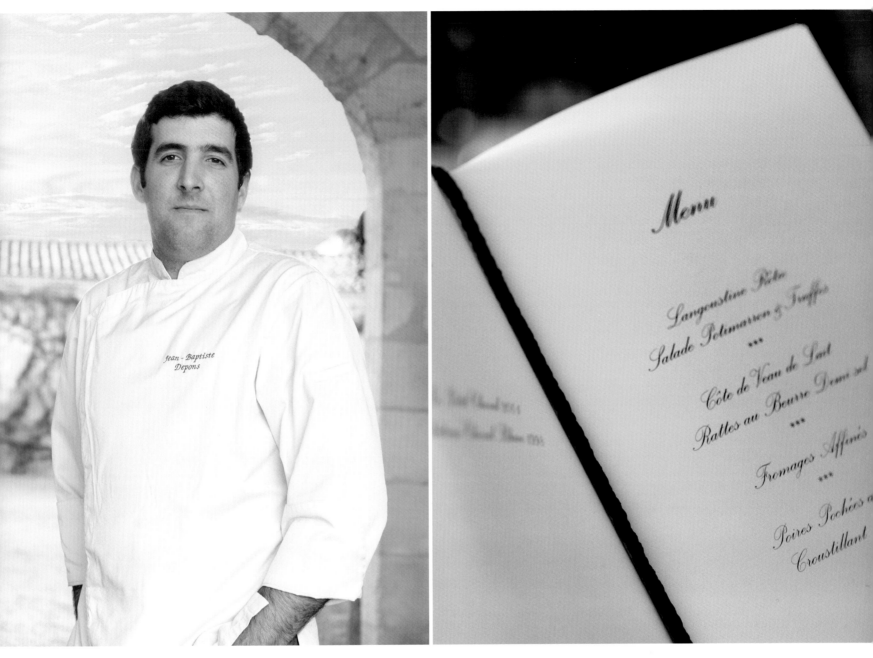

THE CHEFS REGULARLY SERVE DARK CHOCOLATE DESSERTS IN THE FORM OF CREAMY CAKES, MOUSSES, CREPES, SHERBETS, AND OTHER DELIGHTS, WED TO CAREFULLY SELECTED VINTAGES FROM THE WINE CELLAR.

PAGE 239, FACING PAGE, AND ABOVE: *Château Cheval Blanc has been ranked* premier grand cru classé A *for over half a century. It manages to create a peerless balance between two noble varieties of grape, Merlot (round, full, velvety) and Cabernet Franc (fresh, fruity, with fine tannins). In the château, dishes devised by chef Jean-Baptiste Depons exalt all the culinary combinations made possible by the wonderful aromatic complexity, silken texture, and fruity freshness of Cheval Blanc.*

CHÂTEAU D'YQUEM

As the night wearies it recedes slowly, leaving behing it a thick mist that daylight struggles to break through. Vague forms slowly become distinguishable: large trees; a dark mass of high, crenellated walls; towers with pointed roofs. Dawn is finally breaking over Yquem. It will be a while before the mist has totally lifted, allowing the tears it has left on the clusters of grapes to dry off. Without this mist, or at the very least a heavy dew, the grapes would not produce Château d'Yquem's *premier cru supérieur*, a Sauternes that is one the finest sweet wine in the world.

The sun and easterly wind have begun to dry the grapes. The horizon becomes visible. In the heart of the Sauternes region, south of Graves, the château on the hill overlooks the Garonne valley— its 180-degree view takes in most of the Bordeaux winemaking realm. But only here, in the vineyards of Sauternes that cover just five municipalities and total only five thousand acres or so is there the mist that triggers a special alchemy, transforming grapes into liquid gold. At Yquem, the morning dampness is produced by the forest of Les Landes, at the southern edge of the property, by the Garonne River to the north, and especially by its small tributary, the Ciron.

Can this be all it takes to produce such a miracle? Obviously not. But, combined with warm autumn breezes, it encourages the growth of a microscopic fungus, *Botrytis cinerea*, more familiarly known as "noble rot." Without this fungus on the grapes, there would be no sweet wine, no Sauternes. This fungus is a parasite common to all vineyards, where it is staunchly resisted because it can turn into "gray rot" and wreak havoc with the grape harvest. In Sauternes however, a number of factors, some of them still very mysterious, come together to create the conditions that allow the fungus to ennoble the grapes, and to concentrate and preserve their qualities. Since this process favors grapes that are already very ripe, it often requires very late harvesting dates.

Botrytis cinerea progressively works its way into the grapes, without stripping the skin, and then begins a process of transformation. It absorbs a grape's water, feeds on acidic elements plus a little sugar, and ultimately leaves an infinitely smooth, concentrated syrup. The process is never guaranteed, however. In addition to some fifty operations that need to be carried out on the vines in winter and summer, favorable climate conditions are required throughout the year: no frost in spring,

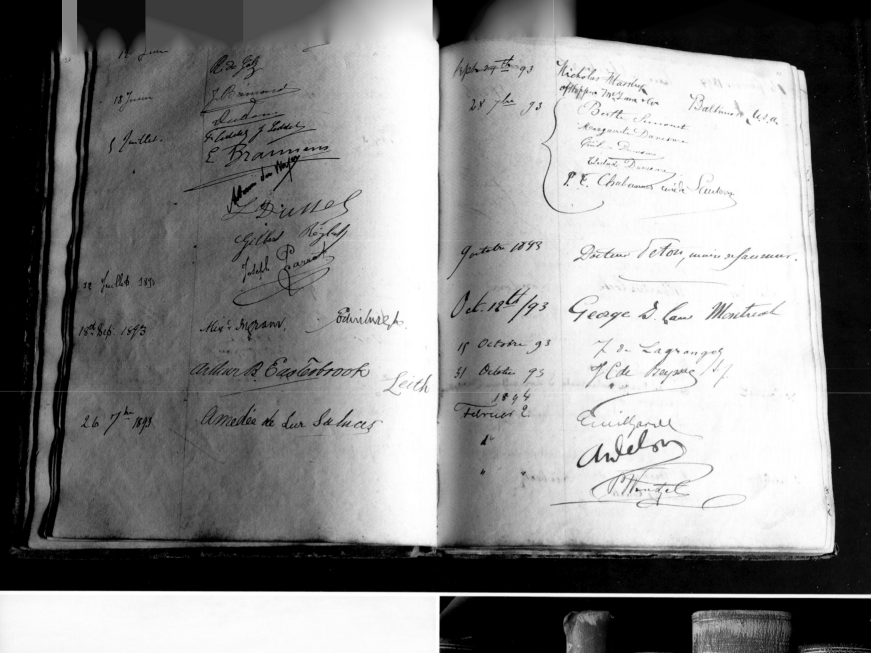

12 Juin   R. de Gilz

18 Juin   J. Brimond

5 Juillet.   Dudon

                           Fidèle J. Liddel

                           E. Brauwers

                           Albert du Halay

                           L. Drouel

                           Gilbert Réglat

                           Joseph Parrot

12 Juillet 1893

18 Sep. 1893   Alex. Ingram   Edinburgh

                          Arthur B. Eastbrook   Leith

26 7br 1893   Amédée de Lur Saluces

Sept 29th 93   Nicholas Marthy   Baltimore U.S.a.
                of Stoppani Metz ma & Co

28 7bre 93   Berthe Surmont

                Marguerite Duresme

                Guil. Duresme

                Edward Duresme

                P. E. Chabannes curé de Sauternes

9 octobre 1893 Docteur Péton, maire de Sauternes.

Oct. 12th/93   George S. Law Montreal

15 Octobre 93   J. de Lagranges

31 Octobre 93   J. C. de Preyssac

1894
Février 2   Emillard

                Andelon

                P. Wendel

not too much rain in summer, and so on. And once the grapes are ripe, the mornings must also be misty and the afternoons windy yet warm. Without all these conditions, plus a few additional, still-unexplained factors, there will be little or no botrytis, hence little or no Yquem.

For how many centuries has this château of mists and mysteries been the source of the most miraculous of nectars? If we knew for sure, Yquem might seem less delicious. Apparently these sweet wines emerged somewhat by accident, nowhere in particular, with no deliberate intention and at no reliable date. Probably by the seventeenth century people had realized that certain unusual circumstances were advantageous, so that from time to time, alongside regular wine, they could produce a few casks of sweet liquor. We know that late harvests were already the norm in Sauternes at the end of the seventeenth century, and by the middle of the eighteenth century winemakers were regularly producing "sweet, syrupy" wines. For Yquem itself, we can go back to the 1780s with certainty.

In the spring of 1787, Thomas Jefferson, U.S. ambassador to France for two years already, traveled south to Bordeaux to visit wine dealers and to taste some of the region's great wines. On his return to Paris, Jefferson wrote directly to the proprietors to place orders for the wines he liked. But he lacked the address for Yquem. In December he asked for help from the American consul in Bordeaux. "I have established correspondences directly with the owners of the best vineyards. It remains for me to do this at Sauterne [sic]. I have therefore written the enclosed letter to M. Diquem [sic], who makes the best of that name, to begin a correspondence on this object, and to ask him for two hundred and fifty bottles of Sauterne of the vintage of 1784." The consul forwarded the letter, informing the future president of the United States that the current owner of d'Yquem was the son-in-law of Laurent Sauvage d'Yquem, the comte de Lur Saluces. Two years later, having completed his term as ambassador and returned to Philadelphia, Jefferson wrote to the count. "The white wine of

Probably by the seventeenth century people had realized that certain unusual circumstances were advantageous, so that from time to time, alongside regular wine, they could produce a few casks of sweet liquor.

Sauternes of your cru, that you were kind enough to send me in Paris in early 1788 has been so well accepted by Americans who know good wines that I am sure that, now that I am back in the United States, my countrymen here will admire them. While I have been here, I have persuaded our President, General Washington, to try a sample. He would like you to send him thirty dozen, sir, and for myself I would like to have ten dozen."

This apparently extraordinary wine ordered in such quantities by leading Americans could only be a syrupy wine. In the tower of the Château d'Yquem, where the most venerable vintages are stored, the oldest wine—a dark amber liqueur—is contained in a bottle with long neck and narrow base. Bottled in the days before labels were invented, the glass is engraved with the following identification: "1787, Château d'Yquem, Th. J." Indeed, Thomas Jefferson asked that his initials be engraved on the bottles he ordered from America.

In 1787 Louis XIV was still on the French throne, and Bordeaux was enjoying the close of its "Golden Century." Capital of the finest vineyards, it was also a major port for colonial trade. It boasted a fine Royal Square, extensive city docks, and a Grand Theater. Some eighty miles to the east, along the Garonne River, a large, handsome, fortified residence overlooked the valley and seemed to protect the acres of vineyards flanking it. A family lived there happily, unaware of the tragedies that loomed. A child had just been born

PAGE 246: *The flower beds with the vineyards in the distance, as seen from the music room.*
PAGE 247: *"It would take you twenty years to gather, through wisdom and knowledge, what one drop of Yquem will give you in an instant," wrote philosopher Michel Serres. The vintage 2001 shown here is known for its intense nose of ripe and dried fruit evolving into notes that are first spicy, then toasty.*
FACING PAGE: *The winery's visitors' books include the signatures of guests down through the centuries (top, and bottom right). The east façade of the château and the old winery (bottom, left).*

at the château, Antoine Marie Amédée. His mother, née Françoise Joséphine Sauvage d'Yquem, was the last direct heir in a line of owners dating back to 1711, when Léon de Sauvage bought the property outright from the king of France. His ancestor Jacques de Sauvage, a royal counselor and treasurer general, had acquired the leasehold in 1593.

The father of the newborn boy, Louis Amédée de Lur Saluces, had probably been a childhood friend of the mother, since the two families were neighbors. The Lur Saluces, whose roots were Franconian on the Lur side and Piedmontaise on the Saluces side, had owned the château de Fargues, located just a few miles from Yquem, since the late fifteenth century.

Tragedy began to strike the estate in on October 1788, when Louis Amédée died suddenly after falling from his horse. Françoise Joséphine would therefore have to confront the events of the 1789 French Revolution on her own. On December 11, 1793, a revolutionary committee conducted a search of the premises and confiscated "titles and feudal and seigniorial documents." The next day, these documents were publicly burned in the town square of Sauternes. On December 14, Françoise Joséphine's father-in-law, Claude Henry de Lur Saluces, was declared "an outlaw, being an aristocrat," and was sentenced to the guillotine by a revolutionary tribunal in Bordeaux. On the following day, Françoise Joséphine herself was arrested. She remained in prison for a month and a half. During that time, on December 26, an inventory was made of "effects belonging to the Lur Saluces at the place called Yquem," a preliminary stage of the official confiscation of the property.

Somehow Françoise Joséphine managed to hold onto Yquem despite everything. How? Maybe she succeeded in proving that her ownership wasn't a feudal heritage, since her great grandfather, Léon de Sauvage, had purchased it. Whatever the case, she must have fought long and hard, alone, demonstrating uncommon strength of character. Another indication of her temperament was the tenacity and passion she put into managing her property. It was she who transformed the estate

Bottled in the days before labels were invented, the glass is engraved with the following identification: "1787, Château d'Yquem, Th. J." Indeed, Thomas Jefferson asked that his initials be engraved on the bottles he ordered from America.

into a true winemaking operation, building in 1826 the wine cellar that made it possible to mature the wines, and that still exists today. It was also Françoise Joséphine who closely monitored the quality of Yquem wine, determined to perpetuate its reputation as the finest of Sauternes. When the official classification of white wines in Gironde was announced in 1855, four years after her death, Yquem was ranked first, the only one to be awarded the grade of *premier cru supérieur*, which it has maintained ever since.

Even nowadays visitors to the Château d'Yquem can still feel the presence of this extraordinary woman who ran the estate for over sixty years. They can see Françoise Joséphine's bedroom, where two windows, facing north and east, still offer a view of the vineyards. The fine little chapel once again offers the freshness of painted scenes that she would have seen when she was married there in 1785, dating probably from the late seventeenth century. They include a Nativity, an Annunciation, and other biblical events inspired by Raphael and Rubens, wonderfully restored between 1998 and 2000. On the ground floor, when the woodwork in the grand salon was being renovated a few years ago, frescoes came to light; they also date from the seventeenth century, and feature hunting scenes, including a bear hunt. They must have reminded Françoise Joséphine of the days when Yquem was still half-wild and still belonged to the king of France. The frescoes have been covered up again: for their own protection, of course, but also to

protect the charm of Yquem, the château of secrets.

Françoise Joséphine's son, Antoine Marie, died young, so it was her grandson, marquis Roman Bertrand de Lur Saluces, who inherited the property. On his death in 1867, he was succeeded by his eldest son, Amédée. Since Amédée died childless, it was his younger brother Eugène who took over the reins. Eugène's son, Bertrand, born in 1888, therefore became lord of Yquem just after World War I. With his sparkling personality, tireless energy, and extensive intellectual cultivation (he spoke half a dozen languages, including fluent Russian), the man known in the region as "the marquis" cultivated the integrity and quality of Yquem without making the least concession to the fashions of the day. For example, he stubbornly refused to add sugar, a perfectly legal process called chaptalization, which he considered a shameful trick. Chairman of the Union des crus classés de la Gironde from 1927, the year the grower's organization was launched, and a founder of the Académie du vin de Bordeaux, the marquis pioneered labels specifying *"mis en bouteille au château,"* or "estate bottled," a guarantee to consumers. And in the late 1950s, he invented "Y," a wonderful dry white wine produced in very small quantities from grapes not selected for Yquem itself. "Y" is a powerful, well-structured wine, similar to Château d'Yquem in its roasted notes, and it is a perfect accompaniment to all cuisine with lively flavors. Bertrand de Lur Saluces died a childless bachelor in 1968.

Two years prior to his death, the marquis called to his side one of his nephews, the comte Alexandre de Lur Saluces, born in 1934. On becoming head of the estate, Alexandre had to face several difficult years for Bordeaux wines. Château d'Yquem was obviously famous throughout the world, but the economic situation made it more complicated to sell the wine. So with great savvy and creativity Alexandre set about helping the public to understand that Yquem is in fact an extraordinary libation. The outstanding, now legendary, vintage of 1975 and the very generous year of 1976 gave a boost to the château's

finances. The 1980s also produced some magnificent years, allowing Alexandre to pursue the development plans he had envisaged.

Earlier financial difficulties had made it impossible to replant sections of vineyards where the old vines had been uprooted. Twelve acres had been lying fallow for a long time. The tractors were aging, and even manuring had to be given up. So investment from the economic upturn went first of all into the renovation of vineyard facilities: a manure container was built, new tractors were bought, thirty thousand grapevines were planted, and three new pneumatic, vertical presses were acquired, yielding better juices. Improved care was given to every stage of winemaking. Château d'Yquem managed to maintain exceptional quality even as output rose from an average of sixty-six thousand bottles per year to eighty thousand bottles around 1980, reaching approximately one hundred thousand bottles in the year 2000.

The most lasting mark of Alexandre's contribution, perhaps, was the building of a new, underground cellar and winery. Dug into a plot unsuited to vine plants, it doubled storage capacity when it was opened in 1987. Its magnificent stone-and-wood staircase leads to a vast, columned crypt that holds hundreds of oak casks. A few years later, the cellar was fitted with blending vats and bottling facilities in order to improve handling. The building of these facilities reflects the highly demanding standard of quality that Alexandre inherited from his uncle. These standards, which guarantee that

When the official classification of white wines in Gironde was announced in 1855, Yquem was ranked first, the only one to be awarded the grade of premier cru supérieur, *which it has maintained ever since.*

FACING PAGE: *Originally built during the Renaissance, the château still resembles a medieval castle in certain ways (top). Here the west gate—like the east gate—is topped by defensive machicolation, tower, and crenellated rampart. A detail from a seventeenth-century fresco depicting a bear hunt, which came to light when the salon was restored (bottom, left). A view of the chapel, inside the château walls (bottom, right).*

Yquem's prestige remains intact, often mean that a good part of the grape harvest has to be rejected—sometimes, the entire harvest is deemed unsatisfactory. No Château d'Yquem at all was produced on nine occasions in the twentieth century, three of them after Alexandre took over the estate—in 1972, 1974, and 1992. Since then, the count has been able to compensate for these poor or non-existent years by constituting large stocks of vintage wine that enable him to satisfy wine merchants' needs and mitigate the loss of income. The new winery therefore represents an additional guarantee of the outstanding quality of Château d'Yquem.

Comte Alexandre de Lur Saluces took Yquem's prestige to great heights by traveling extensively, by sparking countless press stories and photo spreads, and by supporting the publication of both scholarly works and lavishly illustrated books for the general public (including Richard Olney's magnificent *Yquem*, translated into many languages and reprinted many times).

The count officially retired in 2004. Five years earlier, in fact, the family had relinquished sole ownership of the estate: when certain heirs wanted to sell their shares, the LVMH group acquired a majority stake in the enterprise. And when Alexandre retired, Pierre Lurton was appointed by LVMH to replace him. Lurton's natural mission was to preserve the almost divine superiority of Château d'Yquem and share it with all those who seek to taste, understand, and love it.

Sharing also means, among other things, making the château more hospitable. In the spring of 2004 a decision was made to renovate it, the better to receive distinguished guests. From preliminary plans to final completion, the project lasted over two years. The restoration was done with the greatest architectural and historical respect for the Château d'Yquem even as new facilities were included for greater comfort and lavishness. Interior designer Olivier Goubot was given the mission of respecting and enhancing the château's original decorative idiom. Relatively modern parquet flooring was thus replaced by Versailles-style parquet. Most of the woodwork was also

Can the morning dampness be all it takes to produce such a miracle? Obviously not. But, combined with warm autumn breezes, it encourages the growth of a microscopic fungus, Botrytis cinerea, *more familiarly known as "noble rot."*

changed: the oak-paneled salon was fitted with Louis-XV style paneling from a mid eighteenth-century residence in Rouen, having been adapted and re-carved by a team of traditional woodworkers. Meanwhile, the paneling in the dining room was newly designed but based on the woodwork in the château de Balleroy, built by the famous architect Mansart during the same period as Yquem—the new woodwork is a perfect match with the large, period fireplace. By the end of 2006, the renovated interior of the château finally offered visitors a setting more appropriate to its history and calling, even while providing peerless comfort.

The grounds, meanwhile, were revamped, beginning with a fine garden of hardy plants above the modern wine cellar. Their bright colors create a harmonious counterpoint to the relative austerity of the seignorial manor. From early spring until late autumn, roses, sage, Japanese anemones, chrysanthemums, and irises blossom in high, colorful flowerbeds ringed by a charming arbor.

A MIRACLE OF NATURE

Yquem is a miracle of nature made possible by human effort. The pride of the dozens of men and women who work this miracle on a day-to-day basis is no lesser than that of the owners or managers. A staff of forty works all year round on the two hundred and forty acres of Sauternes-graded vineyard (the estate covers four hundred and fifty acres, including woods and meadows). Most

PAGES 254–255: *The vaulted ceiling of the chapel boasts frescoes on biblical subjects inspired by Raphael and Rubens, probably dating from the late seventeenth century.*
FACING PAGE: *There can be no Yquem without* Botrytis cinerea, *a microscopic fungus that feeds on the acids and water in grapes, leaving behind a thick, sweet concentrate. That is why the fungus is called "noble rot," as seen on the dried, withered grapes on this bunch. Every grape affected by botrytis must be picked without delay.*

employees are following in the footsteps of their parents and grandparents. During the grape harvest, some one hundred and eighty people work the vines, most of them from the local area, ready to run to Yquem the moment the picking has to start.

There the first task of winegrowers is to preserve the land, the same way an artwork requires preservation by a museum. The land needs protecting, its integrity needs respecting, and its qualities need to be brought to the fore. The relatively poor soil on the slopes of Yquem is nevertheless rich enough to never require fertilizer apart from a little manure spread over the plots once every five years. This manure is composed of a special straw brought from the Gers region, then distributed to local livestock farmers. Nor is any weed-killer used at Yquem; instead, several shallow plowings eliminate unwanted growth. The land at Yquem is unique in the world. Or perhaps one should say lands, for the vineyards (largely a mixture of clay, sand, and pebbles which create the region's famous *graves*, or slopes of stony gravel, which favor drainage, and aerate the soil) form a palette or mosaic, described by Francis Mayeur, Yquem's technical director (and living memory) since 1983, as a stack of plates arranged upside-down, slightly tilted, and broken. The various layers therefore do not always sit at the same depth on all the one hundred and fifty individual plots. Each plot has its own special character, each producing a different grape; wherever possible, each is tended by the same person year after year. Most of these plots would yield excellent Sauternes, but Château d'Yquem is the fruit of highly skilled blending, or *assemblage*.

The staff assigned to the vines have fifty-one tasks to carry out on the plants throughout the year. Just as the relative poverty of the soil must be respected, so it seems that the most important instruction issued to the vineyard workers is to produce the finest, and therefore *smallest*, yield possible. Whereas the legally authorized yield for Sauternes vineyards is twenty-five hectoliters of wine per hectare of land (roughly 270 gallons per acre) the average at Yquem has been just ten hectoliters over the past twenty years (108 gallons per acre). A more striking image, perhaps, is the one that inevitably comes to mind as you stroll through the rows of grapevines at Yquem: if all goes well, each plant will produce just one glass of wine. The paradox of this wonderfully generous parsimony is not hard to grasp, because without it a glass of Yquem, that powerful concentrate of natural properties and human genius, would not be such a rich experience.

The crucial task is the winter pruning. This hard, very precise pruning basically involves eliminating some of the shoots of the previous years with hand cutters, and cutting back on the remaining shoots so that future growth will not exceed former growth. In the spring, the vines are thinned again when undesirable shoots are nipped with two fingers. The clusters of grapes that appear after flowering are therefore few and far between, but the entire nutrition of the plant must go into them; this calls for further trimming in July, so that the sap of new leaves is directed straight to the burgeoning fruit. The final operation prior to the harvest entails cutting back the leaves of the vine, an operation that requires experience and attention and that is said to be like undressing an angel! This is done so that the grapes are exposed to the autumn sun and so that the noble rot spreads easily. But only east-facing leaves are cut away, so the grapes will dry in the morning sun yet remain sheltered from rains arriving from the west. Gradually, botrytis sets into some of the grapes. The skin becomes patchy with tiny spots, then turns brown, withers, and wrinkles. If sampled, such grapes already taste a little like sultanas or raisins, though with a much greater aromatic range. The level of sugar in these grapes will produce an alcohol level of twenty or twenty-one degrees. Such grapes must be picked right away, even though a neighboring grape may still be green, requiring more sun and more rot, while others may have "turned bad" with gray rot, and must therefore be discarded.

That is why harvest-time at Yquem is called "selection." The successive selections usually begin in the latter half of September, and in theory continue for six weeks. Sometimes they may begin as early as August 28, such as in the year 1893, or finish as late as December 19, as in 1985. Sometimes selection may last just nine days, as happened after the heat wave of the summer of 2003. Nothing is predictable here, for everything depends on the vagaries of the weather. And nothing is simple or straightforward, because each plot develops differently. Everything is costly, because all the pickers must be available at all times, even when nothing happens; furthermore, picking is done even on Sundays when necessary. The decision to pick is made on a day-by-day, even hour-by-hour, basis, and sometimes everything may come to a sudden halt if rain arrives, since the grapes cannot be harvested wet. Thus every plot is subjected to four, five, or six "selections," or even as many as eleven, like the catastrophic year of 1964 when, despite Herculean efforts to obtain a few decent grapes, no Yquem was produced.

There is no point in picturing the usual hod, or large back-basket typically seen in French vineyards: when a picker arrives at the end of a row at Yquem, the volume of withered grapes and clusters is so modest that it fits comfortably into a light poplar wood basket, whose joins are ritually sealed with wax prior to the harvest, so that not a single drop of the precious syrup will be lost. The fruit from the plot are placed in a larger wooden tub, raising a light cloud of dust, after close checking and sorting by an experienced hand; then without delay, a tractor shuttles them to the winery in small quantities. There, by a curious twist of fate, in the courtyard of a fine building erected next to the château in the early nineteenth-century by Françoise Joséphine herself, the harvested grapes are now met by another woman, who sends them on the long path leading to the bottle. The

oenologist Sandrine Garbay has been the master winemaker at Yquem since 1997. Her first task is to inspect the grapes, assessing their texture and fragility in order to determine the right setting for the winepresses.

The grapes undergo four pressings. Unlike

Whereas the legally authorized yield for Sauternes vineyards is twenty-five hectoliters of wine per hectare of land (roughly 270 gallons per acre) the average at Yquem has been just ten hectoliters over the past twenty years (108 gallons per acre).

almost all other wines, the level of sugar and the quality of the juice increase with successive pressings. Oak casks, holding two hundred twenty-five liters (sixty gallons), are then filled with the wonderful golden liquid, and fermentation begins. Depending on the quality of the "must," as the pressed juice is called, fermentation will last from two to six weeks. After this fermentation, the level of alcohol is at 12.5 to 14.5°. The harvest from each day is then matured separately in barrels for six to eight months. In the spring following the harvest, an initial evaluation of the various batches is made; the wines are tasted and analyzed. Some will be judged unworthy of the Yquem label and will be pitilessly rejected. Under certain conditions, they may later be marketed under a generic Sauternes label, or sometimes even distilled into eau-de-vie. The worthy candidates, meanwhile, will undergo a first blending process, then will be returned to casks and placed in the maturing cellar, where they will spend thirty months on average. Those thirty months involve intensive care—a weekly topping-up, which involves refilling the casks to the brim in order to minimize contact with

FACING PAGE: *A nighttime view of the courtyard, with the well in the center (top). Each grape picker is given a light poplar wood basket whose joins have been sealed with wax in order to avoid losing a single drop of the precious syrup (bottom, left). Oenologist Sandrine Garbay, seen here in the tasting room, has been cellar master at Yquem since 1998 (bottom, right). She shapes the personality of each vintage.* PAGES 262–263: *Casks in the wine cellar built in 1987. The wine from the year's harvest will age here in casks for an average of thirty months before being bottled.*

Château d'Yquem is the most accomplished wine
from Sauternes. It's a constant marvel. It displays exceptional
aromatic complexity while maintaining peerless equilibrium
in the mouth. You might think that nothing could be improved—
which is what I assumed before I started this job. Nothing could be
further from the truth. Especially with a *grand cru*—with a wine as
exceptional as Château d'Yquem you have to constantly challenge
yourself, always try to do better. You can always better a technique
in order to attain a new supremacy. The ability to spark new
perceptions is in fact what characterizes a great wine.
For me, the harvest period is the most stimulating part
of the year, because you witness the birth of a vintage year
with its own identity. But assemblage is obviously the most creative
moment, when the true personality of the wine emerges.
You never weary of it.

———————

Sandrine Garbay
CELLAR MASTER

Tasting notes

VINTAGE: 2009
HARVEST: Two very hot weeks in mid August accelerated the ripening of the grapes, followed by mild rain
at the end of the month that insured the uniform spread of Botrytis cinerea. By late September they were
darkening and had attained an ideal state of "noble rot." The grape pickers raced against the clock from
October 1 to October 19, the goal being to pick each individual plot at its best moment. The harvest was
superb, so the only challenge was to avoid an over-concentration of sugar.
FIRST NOSE: A veritable bowl of fruit and spices with refreshing floral overtones.
ATTACK IN MOUTH: Intense, silky, long lasting.
PERFECT COMBINATIONS: Lobster and crayfish; fish in a white sauce, fowl, and game; veined cheeses;
and simple desserts made with fresh fruit.

air; plus ten successive "rackings," designed to remove sediments. During this maturing process, the wines are subjected to blind tastings and some of them will be eliminated.

During the third winter, the wine is finally drawn from the casks and bottled. The bottles are made of clear glass, the better to appreciate the color of the nectar and its evolution from pale gold to deep amber over the years. The corks are unusually long, fifty-four millimeters (2 1/4 inches), because, even though the Yquem is already marvelous, it is designed to last for eternity. Then there is the white label with its trimmed corners and gold letters and borders, probably devised by Françoise Joséphine to convey the purity and grace that weds container to content.

Yquem is an illuminating wine, in the way that ideas are illuminating, suddenly revealing a truth. This ambrosia does not require a learning process or long explanation in order to be loved. It is so different from other wines that it is unfailingly identified during blind tastings. One need not even be an expert taster to recognize it, although connoisseurs will distinguish aromas of candied citrus fruit, of pear or apple jam, of cinnamon, quince, apricot, honey, and so on, depending on the vintage. In one of the finest descriptive evocations of Yquem ever written, French philosopher Michel Serres listed in his 1985 essay on the five senses: "spring flowers, eglantine and lilac, clematis, plus summer fruit including peaches, and autumn or winter fruit such as pears, apples, grapes, and walnuts, with hazelnuts rolling in behind, along a wood dark with ferns, and suddenly truffles in the gray humus, and bark sticky with resin, then rare mineral fragrances of silex, flint, and animal scents, musk, and amber...." Serres carries on for a full page, and every word of what he wrote is probably true. But in the end, maybe it was the French novelist Frédéric Dard who was right when he stated, in his fine foreword to Olney's book, that it is pointless to write about the taste of Yquem because, "Words cannot keep up. Words simply do

During the third winter, the wine is finally drawn from the casks and bottled. The bottles are made of clear glass, the better to appreciate the color of the nectar and its evolution from pale gold to deep amber over the years.

not exist, in any language, to express the infinite pleasure that is offered up." What might be said, at least tentatively, is that Yquem delivers to the nose and palate sensations so smooth and harmonious, so rich and yet so perfectly balanced, somewhere between sweetness and sharpness, vegetal and mineral, that its long-lasting delicious flavor seems destined for all of humankind.

It has often been said that Yquem is part of humanity's heritage in the same way as other valued treasures of nature and history. It is loved all over the world, and has been loved for centuries. Writers such as Turgenev and Colette have sung its praises. In *Backwards to Britain*, Jules Verne referred to Yquem when one of his characters, Edmond, has his friends "taste a certain Lur Saluces of which he cannot speak without exposing himself."

To what do we expose ourselves in the presence of Yquem? To the sacred, as Yquem inspires lofty words indeed. Once again, Frédéric Dard talks of its "enchantment," a word that must be savored deeply, like the wine to which it alludes. An enchantment— from the same root as incantation "casting a spell"—is magic that is supernatural and beneficial in nature, performing wonders like Merlin the Magician. "Take the region of Sauternes," wrote Serres, "with its vineyards and woods, pines and flowers, river and breezes: it would take you twenty years to gather, through wisdom and knowledge, what one drop of Yquem will give you in an instant."

Purists would say that this extraordinary instant suffers no compromise, and that it should always be enjoyed without food. Yet the classic marriage of Yquem with an excellent foie gras, when two textures caress one another so sensually, is another of those eternal moments. Some people also appreciate Yquem with oysters, although vinegar must be avoided at all costs. Nothing prevents Yquem, on the other hand, from accompanying white meat, delicate fish dishes, or lobster. The château's official chef, Marc Demund, often orchestrates reinvented versions of local cuisine. He feels that the most important thing is to avoid "disturbing" the wine, which means excluding dishes that have too much acidity, herbs, condiments, or bitterness, as well as overly sugary desserts. Given those simple rules, anything goes—except red meat. As the high priest in the holy of holies, Demund has the privilege of using Yquem itself in his sauces: once reduced and made moderately creamy, an Yquem sauce is somewhat acid in a way that evokes Asian cuisine.

Demund often dazzles his guests with combinations that are both classic and unforgettable. Certain cheeses are a true delight, such as mature Comté, or creamy blue cheeses, or even a distinguished Roquefort. The problems begin to arise with desserts: since too much sweetness must be avoided, Yquem tolerates only a dessert based on citrus fruit, or a fruit pie, or certain almond-based treats. Another issue to be resolved is finding the right wine that can follow a first course accompanied by Yquem. Almost none are suitable, in fact. A solution to this problem exists, however, and is occasionally followed at the château: after the first course and the first Yquem, a hot or lukewarm broth is served, thereby neutralizing the deliciously persistent flavors on the taste buds; subsequently some other grand wine can be served without scruple. But this gastronomic experience is reserved for just a few special guests at the château. Counting breakfasts, lunches, and dinners, only a hundred meals are served over the year in honor of privileged Yquem merchants and enthusiastic connoisseurs.

On June 19, 2005, an exceptional event brought nearly five hundred guests to the château: the celebration of the 150th anniversary of the Bordeaux vintage classification system. Food journalists, wine experts, and leading wine stewards from all over the world, as well as vineyard owners and their friends, enjoyed a meal under a large glass structure specially erected on the grounds. Four great chefs devised a meal that showcased the finest wines of Médoc, Sauternes, and Barsac—Ken Holmes masterminded hors-d'oeuvres (discussed below), Michel Guérard prepared the first course, Jean-Pierre Biffi did the main course, and Michel Trama devised a dessert. This latter—a vanilla-and-honey jelly with wild strawberries—was accompanied by the apotheosis of the meal, namely one of the finest vintages of the twentieth century, Yquem 1967.

Outside the château, a few other great chefs habitually work with Yquem. Yannick Alléno, the three-star chef at Le Meurice in Paris, patiently familiarized himself with the complexity of Yquem before venturing into original combinations of new recipes and vintage Yquems. Alléno feels that the main thing is to underscore the wine, to bring out its richness. For example, an early tasting of a vintage 2009 with its freshness and hint of saltiness inspired him to create a beef dish in aspic with caviar and watercress sauce. A truly great 1947, meanwhile, with its buttery notes and exceptional yet fresh sweetness gave him the idea of mascarpone with licorice and lemon served with hot, buttery little madeleines. Alléno also likes challenges, so despite the difficulty of marrying a wine to artichokes, he discovered that this vegetable can bring out the overtones of hazelnut in certain Yquems. Other experiments entailed playing on the serving temperature of the wine, the better to bring out certain notes of its aromatic palette. He constantly comes up with other original, subtle

FACING PAGE: *The wine cellar beneath the château holds the oldest wines, including the 1861 vintage, which has never left the estate. Sampled twice, it reveals all the vitality, depth, and complexity of a great vintage.*

THE IMAGINATION, EXPERIMENTATION, AND RESPECTFUL BOLDNESS THAT YANNICK ALLÉNO BRINGS TO THE ART OF SERVING YQUEM HAVE GIVEN BIRTH TO A SMALL LAB, OR WORKSHOP.

ABOVE: *Yannick Alléno is the three-starred chef at Hotel Le Meurice in Paris (left). His bold and fertile yet rigorous talent has devised culinary combinations that bring out the profound aromatic complexity of Yquem. Vintage 1896 has a highly complex bouquet of candied fruit that offers a world of inspiration to Alléno (right).*

FACING PAGE: *The heady flavors of curried lobster with saffron and ginger lend their spicy aromas to the smooth sweetness of a Château d'Yquem 2001, whose nose of ripe and candied fruit develops into spicier, toasty notes.*

Chef Yannick Alléno's Recipe

CURRIED LOBSTER AND CLAWS
IN SMALL RAVIOLI WITH SPICED BROTH

INGREDIENTS

Serves 4

· 4 lobsters, about 1 lb. (500 g) apiece

Lobster Broth:
· 4 lobster heads
· 2 teaspoons (10 ml) olive oil
· 1 carrot
· 2 Roma tomatoes
· ½ onion
· 1 stick celery
· 2 cups (500 ml) fish fumet
· ⅔ oz. (20 g) chopped ginger

Curry Sauce:
· ½ white onion
· 2 teaspoons (10 ml) olive oil
· ½ Granny Smith apple
· 1 teaspoon curry powder
· 1 pinch saffron threads
· 5 cardamom seeds

· 3 tablespoons (50 ml) coconut milk
· Scant ½ cup (100 ml) lobster broth

Lobster and Shrimp Ravioli:
· 4 lobster claws
· 3 ½ oz. (100 g) small grey shrimp (*crevettes grises*)
· 1 teaspoon (5 g) chopped ginger
· 1 teaspoon (5 g) chopped galangal
· 1 tablespoon unsalted butter, softened
· ¾ cup (100 g) flour
· 1 egg yolk
· 1 tablespoons plus 2 teaspoons (25 ml) water
· 1 pinch (1 g) saffron threads

Ginger Butter:
· Scant ½ cup (100 ml) lobster broth

· 1 very small knob (5 g) ginger
· 3 tablespoons (50 g) unsalted butter

Garnish:
· 1 Granny Smith apple
· 1 lime
· 1 mango
· 1 coconut
· 1 sprig Thai chives
· 8 orange baby carrots
· 8 bok choy leaves

Finish and presentation:
· 3 ½ oz. (100 g) fatback
· 4 new onions
· Scant ½ cup (100 ml) whole milk
· 2 tablespoons (20 g) flour
· 2 tablespoons (20 g) curry powder
· 1 tablespoon plus 1 teaspoon (20 ml) olive oil

METHOD

Separate the lobster tails from the heads (use the heads to make the broth). Reserve the largest claw of each lobster and reserve the second largest for the ravioli.

Lobster broth: Crush the lobster heads and sauté them with olive oil. Roughly dice the carrot, tomatoes, onion, and celery. Cover with fish fumet and simmer gently over low heat for 1 hour, skimming regularly. Strain through a fine-meshed chinois. Add the chopped ginger and let it infuse for 10 minutes. Strain the broth through cheesecloth and keep warm over a hot water bath.

Curry Sauce: Chop the half onion and sweat it in olive oil. Chop the apple and add it to the pan with the spices. Let stew gently. Cover with the coconut milk and lobster broth. Simmer over low heat for 10 minutes. Process in a blender and strain through a fine-meshed chinois. Keep warm over a hot water bath.

Lobster and Shrimp Ravioli: To make the stuffing, chop the claws and shelled shrimp. Combine the chopped ginger and galangal with the butter, and mix in the chopped lobster and shrimp.

(CONTINUED ON PAGE 277)

Château Yquem

du 11 janvier 2012

de Mâche

Fis

uses of Yquem, such as aging a piece of beef in an old Yquem cask that still contains a little wine. The imagination, experimentation, and respectful boldness that Alléno brings to the art of serving Yquem shoud give birth to a small lab, or workshop, dubbed *La Table d'Yquem*. This little temple in the basement of Le Meurice—a single table with ten place-settings—would not only be dedicated to the great wine but would also allow guests to watch Alléno's brigade at work behind a glass screen. They thereby participate in a friendly, sophisticated and delectable rite: a meal of truly new culinary harmonies orchestrated around the most famous of Sauternes.

Ken Hom, the famous American chef who launched the Western world's love affair with the *wok*, has long meditated on the best way to combine Yquem with his native Chinese gastronomy. In this respect, his ideas are resolutely non-conformist, indeed revolutionary. He feels that mildly spicy Chinese dishes, rather than harming the wine, resonate very harmoniously with the velvety sweetness of Yquem. The sugar balances the spices. Hom advocates, for example, the marriage of Yquem with ginger or Szechuan pepper. Food cooked at high temperature in a *wok* acquires grilled and smoky notes that are also very harmonious with Sauternes. The only Chinese culinary habits to avoid at all costs are the use of vinegar and overly fatty recipes. For the 150th anniversary of the official Bordeaux vintage classification system, Hom composed the hors-d'oeuvres served with various wines from Sauternes and Barsac. For this glamorous occasion he prepared four recipes that also go well with Yquem: chicken spring rolls with candied orange and coriander, chives, and spring onions; dumplings with chestnuts, Parma ham, and crayfish flavored with sherry and ginger; caramelized pecans; and a pork and chicken consommé seasoned with spring onions, garlic and ginger.

Ken Hom, the famous American chef who launched the Western world's love affair with the wok, has long meditated on the best way to combine Yquem with his native Chinese gastronomy.

Although the music of Yquem is perhaps best appreciated in the glass as it is brought to the lips, it can also be heard while wandering through the château from room to room, when the old floorboards creak and footsteps resound. Or when musing in the vineyard, leaning against the large chestnut tree planted by patients treated there during World War I, and suddenly a bell tolls announcing a pause in the day's labor. Because Yquem is not only a precious nectar, it is also a place, a venerable mount, on which the pleasures of the five senses mingle, especially at that time in autumn when the mist lifts and the roses appear. In olden days, roses—more fragile than grapevines—were planted in vineyards to warn of the danger of disease. On a misty morning, roses are the first to show their colors at the end of a row of vines. Like the grapes, they are dappled with dew. And from this dew is born the nectar of roses, Yquem. This time in the morning recalls another very ancient music, the music of the silken, flowing verse of Joachim du Bellay, the sixteenth century French poet of love, mystery, and metaphysics:

Qui a pu voir la matinale rose
D'une liqueur céleste emmiellée
Quand sa rougeur de blanc entremêlée
Sur le naïf de sa branche repose...

Whoever has seen the morning rose
O'er-honeyed with heavenly dew
Blush pink, yet brushed with white anew,
Upon the simple branch she chose....

PAGES 273 AND 274–275: *In the elegant, seventeenth-century setting of the large dining room, a few select guests are invited to share the unparalleled art of savoring Yquem.*
FACING PAGE: *"Y" was created in 1959. It is made from Yquem grapes that have not been affected by noble rot. Powerful yet delicate, its light roasted aromas are evocative of Yquem. Frédéric Dard has described the tasting of different vintages of Château d'Yquem as the "apotheosis of taste."*

Season with salt and pepper and chill.
To make the ravioli dough, place the flour in a round-bottomed mixing bowl. Make a well and add the egg yolk, water, and saffron. Mix until a smooth dough forms. With a laminator, make two very thin layers. Place twelve small mounds of lobster stuffing on one sheet of dough. Cover with the second sheet of dough and press down between the mounds to seal the two layers together. With a 2 ¼-inch (6-cm) pastry ring or cookie cutter, cut out twelve rounds. Use your fingers to fold the ravioli over.

Ginger Butter: Mix the ingredients for the ginger butter together and keep warm over a hot water bath

Garnish: Finely dice the apple. Place the dice in a bowl of water with a little lime juice and chill.

With a small scoop, prepare balls of mango and place them in the refrigerator.

Break the coconut and separate the flesh from the shell. With a mandoline, make thin slices and cut them into triangles. Cut the Thai chives into angled slices and keep warm over a hot water bath.

Peel the carrots. In boiling salted water, blanch the carrots, chives, and bok choy. Refresh and place in the refrigerator.

To Finish and Present: Freeze the fatback briefly so that it is easy to slice. Slice it very thinly using a meat slicer. With a mandolin, cut the onions into slices just under ⅛ inch (3 mm) thick. Dip them in the milk, drain them, then dip them in the flour combined with the curry powder. Fry them at 285°F (140°C).

Cut the lobster tails in two lengthwise and sear them, shell side down, in a sauté pan with olive oil. Prise the shell from the tail, keeping it attached. Glaze the lobster tails in the ginger butter and top with the fatback.

Cook the ravioli for 3 minutes in boiling salted water. Pan fry the vegetables and large lobster claws.

Draw out a circle of curry sauce in the center of a flat plate. Arrange the finely diced apple, mango scoops, coconut triangles, chives, and fried onions in the plate. Sprinkle curry powder around the rim of the plate and add the lobster tails.

In a soup plate, arrange the vegetables, ravioli, and large lobster claws. Serve the broth in a jug.

ACKNOWLEDGMENTS

The publisher would like to thank the teams at Moët Hennessy, Moët & Chandon,
Mercier, Dom Pérignon, Veuve Clicquot, Krug, Ruinart, Hennessy,
Château Cheval Blanc and Château d'Yquem, all of whom helped to make
this book possible. Special thanks go to Françoise Pottier and Antoine Cohen-Potin
for their efficient coordination and assistance.

Warm acknowledgments for several of the photographs
published here go to the wonderfully hospitable staff
at the following establishments in Paris: Hôtel George V, Hôtel Le Meurice,
Le Train Bleu (Gare de Lyon), and Le Pavillon Elysée Lenôtre.

FACING PAGE: *Gabriele Salci,* Frutta, Cristalle e strumenti musicali con
pappagallo, *the prince of Liechtenstein's collection, Vaduz, Vienna.*

Photographic Credits
t: top, b: bottom, l: left, r: right
All photographs in this book were taken by Francis Hammond with the exception of the following:
Moët & Chandon pp. 24 and 25: © ministère de la Culture-médiathèque du Patrimoine, Dist. RMN-Grand Palais / François Kollar.
Mercier pp. 46 and 47: © Erik Sampers for Champagne Mercier; p. 48t: © Dumelié-Poyet collection / Centre régional de la Photographie de Champagne-Ardenne; p. 48br: © Paulus / Michel Jolyot (reproduction); pp. 52 and 53: © Champagne Mercier collection.
Dom Pérignon pp. 64 and 65: © Keiichi Tahara for Dom Pérignon; p. 70l: © Michael Kenna / Dom Pérignon collection; p. 72t: © RMN (musée du Louvre) / Gérard Blot; p. 72bl: © RMN (château de Versailles) / Franck Raux; pp. 74 and 75: © RMN (château de Versailles) / All Rights Reserved.
Veuve Clicquot p. 103: © Veuve Clicquot archives.
Krug pp. 126br, 128 and 129: © Krug collection; pp. 136, 137 and 139br: © Michel Labelle for Krug.
Ruinart p. 158bl: © Ruinart archives; pp. 164 and 165: © RMN-GP (domaine de Chantilly) / René-Gabriel Ojéda ; p. 171t: © Leif Carlsson ; pp. 171bl and br: © Ruinart archives.
Hennessy pp. 194 and 195: © Hennessy collection; p. 203: © Leif Carlsson.
Château Cheval Blanc pp. 216 and 217: © François Poincet; p. 239: © Lucile Aigron.
Château d'Yquem p. 266: © Jean-Marc Tingaud.
Acknowledgments p. 278: © Liechtenstein / The Princely Collections, Vaduz, Vienna.

Executive Director
Suzanne Tise-Isoré
Styles & Design Collection

Editorial Coordination
Aurélie Hagen-Bastelica

Editorial Assistance
Lucie Lurton

Graphic Design
Isabelle Ducat
assisted by Claude-Olivier Four
for the English version

Translation from the French by
Deke Dusinberre
(main texts, captions and tasting notes)
Carmella Abramowitz Moreau
(recipes)

Copyediting
Helen Woodhall

Color Separation and Printing
Musumeci, Italy

FSC
www.fsc.org
MIX
Paper from
responsible sources
FSC® C102788

Simultaneously published in French as *L'Esprit des vignobles*
© Flammarion S.A., Paris, 2012

English-language edition
© Flammarion S.A., Paris, 2012

Flammarion, S.A.
87, quai Panhard et Levassor
75647 Paris Cedex 13
editions.flammarion.com

12 13 14 3 2 1
ISBN : 978-2-08-020137-9
Dépôt légal : 10/2012